MW01181362

LINEAGE-LINE AND LEGACY

THE POWER TO TRANSFORM A GENERATION

REVISED 2ND EDITION

BY BOBBY CONNER

Lineage-Line and Legacy
Revised 2nd Edition
Copyright 2015 by Bobby Conner
All rights reserved.

Distributed by: Eagles View Ministries

A division of Bobby Conner Demonstration of God's Power Ministries

P.O. Box 933

Bullard, Texas 75757 USA

www.bobbyconner.org

ISBN 978-0-9801639-0-2 Second Printed in United States of America

CONTENTS

My frame was not hidden from You when I was being formed in secret [and] intricately and curiously wrought [as if embroidered with various colors] in the depths of the earth [a region of darkness and mystery]. Your eyes saw my unformed substance, and in Your book all the days [of my life] were written before ever they took shape, when as yet there was none of them. How precious and weighty also are Your thoughts to me, O God! How vast is the sum of them! If I could count them, they would be more in number than the sand. When I awoke, [could I count to the end] I would still be with You.

Ps. 139:15-18 AMP

AUTHOR PROFILE

Bobby and Carolyn Conner are founder and President of Eagles View Ministries (EVM), a global outreach that focuses on revealing a demonstration of God's power—"Empowering the Body of Christ to Take Dominion." Their goal is to prepare an overcoming generation that transcends gender and age, raising the standard of purity and power in order to transform nations. Sounding the alarm, they are awakening the warriors to arise and contend for the true faith, advancing the King in His Kingdom.

Bobby and Carolyn have been married for over fifty years. They have two sons and, five wonderful grandchildren. They pastored Southern Baptist churches for twenty-seven years, and they have been ministering for almost five decades in over fifty nations across the earth!

They are passionate and inspired by a global vision for establishing the Kingdom of God in a true demonstration of God's power, knowing that the Kingdom does not consist of mere words, but of Holy Spirited–empowered works (see **1 Cor. 4:20**). Bobby and Carolyn are on a mission to fulfill the Kingdom-empowerment mandate of Heaven. Bobby has authored numerous books, and he has averaged speaking five times a week for over four and half decades; together, they have a burning passion to spread the uncompromised message of the Kingdom of God to every nation.

You can discover more about
their ministry at
www.bobbyconner.org.

A good name is better than precious ointment.
Ecclesiastes 7:1

INTRODUCTION

Welcome! To Lineage–line and Legacy revised second edition. Within these pages you will discover numerous fresh new insights to assist you in your journey. You will be guided and directed how to release God's Divine spoken blessing over yourself as well as your descendants. You will discover the power to break family curses. Each one of us has been given a priceless gift—the power to influence lives.

For a number of years, the Lord has been urging me regarding writing this book. He has emphasized the significance and consequences of lineage-line and legacy. A deeper understanding of these two aspects of your life will change your entire family line. The potential to shape the generations to come rests upon our shoulders; we have the power to transform lives—our own and those of our descendants.

With in the pages of this book you will be guided and instructed how to release a blessing upon your lineage not just for now, but for years to come. Also you will gain valuable guidelines for breaking lineage-line curses.

It is a proven fact our lives can be the building blocks for overwhelming success or the stumbling stones for coming generations. Take heart, even if you have failed in the past to present a positive encouraging example, it is never too late. Our God can restore and bring about restoration. No situation is too hard for Him:

Is anything too hard for the Lord?
Genesis 18:14

In the 1600s, the poet John Donne wrote the famous phrase, "*No man is an island.*" It is still true today. Simply stated, this means that our actions have an effect upon others. This influence can be for good or for bad, for help or for heartache.

Legacy deals with *what* you leave behind. Lineage-line speaks of *who* you leave behind. Both are connected to the other. Legacy exposes lifestyle and what type of reputation you pass down. Your lineage is composed of your descendants.

Never doubt for a moment that your lineage-line is directly affected by your legacy. How you conduct your life will affect not only you, but also your children and their children for a long time—either for righteous behavior or for a wicked lifestyle. In these pages you will discover how to break family curses, and speak and impart Godly blessings upon your entire lineage-line.

This truth bears repeating over and over. We must realize that how we live our lives *will* affect our family line. In this book, you will discover that each of us has a divine destiny and that our descendants will be greatly blessed if we honor and obey the will of God for our lives.

God not only promises to bless you as you commit to love and obey Him, but He also promises to bless your children and your children's children, even up to the thousandth generation. This type of spiritual investment is truly worth our very best effort.

Your life will be encouraged and inspired as you discover the power of blessing. You will gain valuable insights pertaining to the proper tools for passing God's blessings and favor on to your descendants. Also, you will gain tools to help you break family line curses.

This book will give you guidelines that will enable you to position yourself to overcome and succeed in every area of life. Please understand it is never too late for change.

Take your time as you read and ponder these Scriptural principles they will truly transform your life, and the lives of your children. May the favor of our Heavenly Father flood your life and the lives of those you touch.

*A good man leaves an inheritance to his children's children,
but the wealth of the sinner is stored up for the righteous.*
Proverbs 13:22

CHAPTER 1

What Is Legacy?

Does It Have Significance For Me?

The first question we will deal with is: What is legacy and does it have any significance for me? Every person on earth has a legacy. The world population has reached well over seven billion. Just as every human on earth has distinct fingerprints, so also each of us has a unique legacy. Legacy can be likened to the footprints of life. Just as footprints in soft sand reveal that someone has passed this way, so too your legacy is evidence that you were here on earth, and it points to your accomplishments. Legacy is the fragrance of your life, which lingers long after you have departed from the room.

How you live your life will have lasting consequences upon your family for generations to come. Scripture declares that you will leave an inheritance to your children and grandchildren:

LINEAGE-LINE AND LEGACY

A good man leaves an inheritance to his children's children, but the wealth of the sinner is stored up for the righteous.
Proverbs 13:22

Let me be perfectly clear, the inheritance most needed is not worldly wealth, money, silver and gold, stocks and bonds, but Godly character. Which is a living example of a Christlike life.

As a sharp chisel applied to stone leaves a mark, so the conduct of our lives leaves an impression for good or bad. We must never forget that we too have power to shape others' lives. That is the way legacy works. Scripture states that we will reap what we have sown.

Do not be deceived, God is not mocked; for whatever a man sows, that he will also reap. For he who sows to his flesh will of the flesh reap corruption, but he who sows to the Spirit will of the Spirit reap everlasting life.
Galatians 6:7-8

One of the fundamental principles of sowing is that we will reap more than we have sown.

They sow the wind. And reap the whirlwind. - Hosea 8:7

For example, a farmer sows a single kernel of corn and expects to reap a stalk bearing ears of corn filled with hundreds of kernels. Upright, godly individuals will be encouraged to know that what they sow in the present will bring a harvest in the future.

Just as a small pebble tossed in a pond results in ripples expanding across the pond, so it is with our lives. The events of our lives can and will have far-reaching results. God's Word encourages us to sow good seeds to reap a righteous harvest.

> *Sow for yourselves righteousness. Reap in mercy; Break up your fallow ground, For it is time to seek the Lord, Till He comes and rains righteousness on you.*
>
> *Hosea 10:12 NJKV*

With this in mind, we must make the noble choice and resolve that our lives will be a blessing and not a burden—that they will reflect the overwhelming grace and mercies of our loving Heavenly Father.

The importance of legacy is revealed in the fact that it is mentioned over two hundred times in Scripture. We must not ignore its significance.

Our goal must be to yield to Christ's leadership so that our lives will be bright beacons to others. We are called as followers of Christ to be radiant bright beacons of light that emanate and reflect God's wonderful redemptive love and light to a hurting world. Christ Jesus reminds us:

> *You are the light of the world. A city that is set on a hill cannot be hidden.*
> *Matthew 5:14 NKJV*

None of us want to become a stumbling block to a single person, especially our own families. We are best able to live as bright godly beacons when we start with our own families, setting forth a godly lifestyle. If we set the right example in word and deed, it will have lasting effects upon our children.

Take this wonderful promise to heart:

> *Train up a child in the way he should go, And when he is old he will not depart from it.*
> *Proverbs 22:6*

Legacy is what we leave behind, even a bequest made in a last will and testament. But much more than words on a page, our legacy is how we have conducted our lives. The deepest desire of my heart is to conduct my life in such a manner that, in years to come, when my name is spoken, my family will not hang their heads in shame, but will be honored and blessed by the testimony and example of an upright, godly life. Ponder this precious promise concerning the importance of a good name.

> *A good name is to be chosen rather than great riches, Loving favor rather than silver and gold.*
> *Proverbs 22:1*

Notice the warning to be serious about our walk with Christ. Let this be your core goal also:

> *This is a faithful saying, and these things I want you to affirm constantly, that those who have believed in God should be careful to maintain good works. These things are good and profitable to men.*
> *Titus 3:8*

At my home I have a small tapestry plaque with a huge statement inscribed: *"Never get so busy making a living that you forget to make a life!"* What brings us the greatest dividends is molding the lives of our children. Providing for them a stable and firm foundation.

Lineage-Line and Legacy

The greatest investment we can make is not in the temporal fleeting possessions of this life but rather ceaseless Christ centered things.

Many are making a tragic mistake seeking to find peace and contentment in the temporal things of this life. Christ Jesus states we should seek first the Kingdom of God then everything else will find its proper place.

> *But seek first the kingdom of God and His righteousness, and all these things shall be added to you.*
> *Matthew 6:33 NKJV*

One of the most important investments you can make is revealing true Christ-like character to your family this is the best legacy.

Some synonyms for *legacy* are: *inheritance, bequest, heritage, gift,* and *birthright.* However, our legacy is far more than just material possessions that we pass down to family members. True legacy speaks of upright values, godly character, and a good name.

> *A good name is better than precious ointment......*
> *Ecclesiastes 7:1 NKJV*

True legacy is of a spiritual nature. The most valuable legacy is what we have stood for and how we have conducted our lives; this forms our reputation.

For this reason we also, since the day we heard it, do not cease to pray for you, and to ask that you may be filled with the knowledge of His will in all wisdom and spiritual understanding; that you may walk worthy of the Lord, fully pleasing Him, being fruitful in every good work and increasing in the knowledge of God;

Col. 1:9-10

In case you're still wondering, *Is my legacy significant?* —The answer is a resounding *yes!* Jesus Christ asked a pointed, powerful question:

"For what profit is it to a man If he gains the whole world, and loses his own soul? Or what will a man give in exchange for his soul?"

Matthew 16:26

At the end of a person's life, the thing that truly matters is not a huge bank account, but a life lived for the glory of God.

LINEAGE-LINE AND LEGACY

Each of us should aspire to live our lives so as to hear these words spoken:

"Well done, good and faithful servant"

Matthew 25:21

In the most profound manner, our legacy has the power to shape and affect others and especially to influence many generations following us in our family lines. Through our love and loyalty to Christ, we have the power to transform not only our own lives, but also the lives of our descendants. How we conduct our lives will pass on wonderful, life-changing blessings or deadly, destructive curses to our family lines. Because we are all receiving a legacy from those who came before us, in this book, we will discuss how to destroy family curses and to restore godly blessing upon our ancestral lines. Again I want to declare it's never too late, God desires to restore and heal.

Depending on whether your lifestyle is virtuous or decadent, your legacy will become either a dangerous stumbling block or a delightful stepping-stone for your descendants. Start right now, this very day, by determining that your life will be a bright light that leads others to a deeper walk with Christ Jesus, not a dark shadow of despair and doom.

Even if you have made some wrong choices and have taken some detours, take heart. God's plans for you are good, and He always makes a way for you to repent and return in order to receive restoration.

For I know the thoughts that I think toward you, says the Lord, thoughts of peace and not of evil, to give you a future and a hope.
Jeremiah 29:11 NKJV

It is a true statement that God's ways are always better and so much higher than our ways.

"For as the heavens are higher than the earth, So are My ways higher than your ways, And My thoughts than your thoughts."
Isaiah 55:9 NKJV

It is never too late to restore God's blessings to your family name; God promises to give you the power of a fresh start.

Therefore, if anyone is in Christ, he is a new creation; old things have passed away; behold, all things have become new.
-2 Corinthians 5:17 NKJV

When we respond to the grace and forgiveness of God He removes and cleanses your life from sin.

If we confess our sins, He is faithful and just to forgive us our sins and to cleanse us from all unrighteousness.

1 John 1:9 NKJV

No matter how dark your past has been, when you respond to Christ Jesus, your future will be filled with light, love, and lasting hope.

"Come now, and let us reason together," Says the Lord, "Though your sins are like scarlet, They shall be as white as snow; Though they are red like crimson, They shall be as wool.

Isaiah 1:18

Don't let the failures and pains of the past keep you from the victories of the future.

Brethren, I do not count myself to have apprehended; but one thing I do, forgetting those things which are behind and reaching forward to those things which are ahead, I press toward the goal for the prize of the upward call of God in Christ Jesus.

Philippians 3:13-14

God's promise is to remove your sins from you as far as the east is from the west and to remember them no more!

As far as the east is from the west, So far has He removed our transgressions from us. As a father pities his children, So the Lord pities those who fear Him.

Psalms 103:12-13

Thank God that, in Christ Jesus, you can have a new beginning and you can experience the power of God's mercies, which are new every morning. God is faithful to forgive when we are faithful to repent.

My soul still remembers And sinks within me. This I recall to my mind, Therefore I have hope. Through the Lord's mercies we are not consumed, Because His compassions fail not. They are new every morning; Great is Your faithfulness.

Lamentations 3:20-23

As you think about this reality, ponder this promise from God:

> *So I will restore to you the years that the swarming locust has eaten, the crawling locust, the consuming locust, and the chewing locust, my great army which I sent among you.*
>
> *Joel 2:25*

God is so good! *(Nahum 1:7 - The Lord is good, A stronghold in the day of trouble; And He knows those who trust in Him.)*

His tender mercies are fresh and new, waiting for you to avail yourself of them by simply asking for forgiveness and guidance. Truly, He is overflowing with lovingkindness and tender mercies.

In *Exodus 34:7 "keeping mercy for thousands, forgiving iniquity and transgression and sin, by no means clearing the guilty, visiting the iniquity of the fathers upon the children and the children's children to the third and the fourth generation"*, we discover the promise of God to extend mercy for thousands—forgiving iniquity, transgression, and sin. However, it also says that He visits the iniquity of the fathers upon the children and the family line to the third and forth generation. The choice is up to us.

God is offering each one of us a fresh start, a clean slate. It is true that sadness and weeping might come in the night. However, overwhelming joy comes in the morning.

> *For His anger is but for a moment, His favor is for life; Weeping may endure for a night, But joy comes in the morning.*
> *Psalms 30:5*

Let's prepare to embrace the dawn of a new day, overcoming the pains and failures of yesterday so that we're ready to face a bright new future.

Accept God's wonderful promise:

> *"For You, Lord, are good, and ready to forgive, and abundant in mercy to all those who call upon You."*
> *Psalm 86:5*

In other words, even if you have rejected God's good plan for your life in the past, now is the time to repent, to open your life anew to God. He *will* answer your cry and restore hope and peace in your life, this is a day of favor.

LINEAGE-LINE AND LEGACY

See **2 Corinthians 6:2 - For He says:**

"In an acceptable time I have heard you, And in the day of salvation I have helped you." Behold, now is the accepted time; behold, now is the day of salvation.

As the Bible clearly outlines, God shows abundant mercy to all who love and obey Him (see **Exodus 20:6**). The substance of our love for God is demonstrated when we honor Him and obey His Word (see **John 14:21-23**). Scripture declares that God loves righteousness and hates evil and wickedness because He knows what sin will do in our lives (see **Psalms 45:7**).

He knows it will destroy us. Sin carries a high price; as the Bible says, the wages of sin is death—separation from God and His love, not just for the present, but also for all eternity (see **Romans 6:23**).

God's love for us is everlasting, and He does not want any of us to be eternally separated from Him (see **1 Timothy 2:4**). Thus, He draws us to Himself with tender cords of kindness (see **Jeremiah 31:3**; and **Hosea 11:4**). Thank God for salvation! And if you haven't yet, call upon Christ today so that you may experience this new life in Him (see **Romans 10:9-13**).

The Significance of Your Legacy

To understand the significance of legacy, let's first look at your value and worth, not just to humankind, but also to Almighty God. The world reached a milestone in 2012—the population of the earth reached over seven billion people. Remarkably, not a single one of these seven billion people are just like you. You are extremely precious and special to God.

You have heard the statement, *"You're one in a million!"* But that's not true. Actually, you're one in seven billion!

You are divinely unique, one of a kind you were created by Almighty God for God. You have value and worth beyond your wildest imagination. All the redemptive things that God has done, He would have done even if you had been the only person who needed them. The truth is, God's great plans started for you before you were ever born. Let the magnitude of this passage in **Psalm 139:13-18** encourage you:

> *You made all the delicate, inner parts of my body and knit me together in my mother's womb. Thank you for making me so wonderfully complex!*

Your workmanship is marvelous—how well I know it.

You watched me as I was being formed in utter seclusion, as I was woven together in the dark of the womb.

You saw me before I was born. Every day of my life was recorded in your book. Every moment was laid out before a single day had passed.

How precious are Your thoughts about me, O God! They cannot be numbered!

I can't even count them; they outnumber the grains of sand! And when I wake up, you are still with me (NLT).

Always remember that you were chosen by God for God; therefore, you have divine purpose. You were chosen by God in eternity *past,* to live in the *present,* to forge the *future* (see **Ephesians 2:10**).

As I mentioned previously, when John Donne wrote, "No man is an island," he was telling the truth! Our lives have a tremendous impact on others, for good or bad, to help them or hurt them. Consider this little question with potentially big results—*"If every person on earth was just like me, what kind of world would this world be?"*

It is a massive mistake to underestimate your God-given potential. Stop thinking that you're not important, that your life is insignificant and does not matter. This type of misguided, erroneous thinking will rob both you and your descendants, and it can even devastate their spiritual destiny. Shake yourself, lift your head, and gain the courage you need to face each day knowing that you have been given divine purpose and will, and consequently, you have power.

Never allow doubt and discouragement to grip your heart again. Certainly, the devil is behind this type of attitude. He knows all too well that if you gain an understanding of your value and worth to God, it will change your whole outlook and transform your entire life. You will begin to live your life according to the way you think about yourself in your heart (see **Proverbs 23:7**).

God Himself has given you life, which means you are inexpressibly valuable and important to Him. You have "friends in high places" (see **John 15:15**). You might protest, "I have no great fortune or large inheritance to pass down to my descendants." But as I said before, the most valuable thing you can bequeath to your children is not gold and silver, precious stones, or stocks and bonds. Such gifts are good, but the best gift is godly character and a good name. This is the true treasure that robbers can't steal and rust can't tarnish (see **Matthew 6:20**).

The entire message of the Bible reveals that the greatest thing you can pass down to your children is not a huge bank account, but rather a godly lifestyle, a good name, and a honest upright character.

Don't underestimate yourself, thinking that you're not significant. Nothing could be more distant from the truth (see **John 3:16**). You matter first and foremost to God. It was His plan to create you and to give you life, and He paid the ultimate price for your redemption (see **1 Peter 1:19**).

God's love for each person is evident in light of the sacrifice God provided to save us. Scripture states that the greatest display of love happens when a person gives up his life for another (see **John 15:13**).

That is exactly what Christ Jesus did for us, when He freely yielded His life for us on the cruel cross. The cross of Christ Jesus is love on display.

Second, not only are you valuable to God, but you matter to others, especially your loved ones. Even if you have not been aware of it, your life has bearing and influence upon people around you. Your life is an open book read by all people (see **2 Corinthians 3:2**).

Clearly, you are important. God has a plan that only you can fulfill (see **Ephesians 2:10**), and you are perfectly tailored for the works that God has prepared for you to accomplish (see **Philippians 2:13**). You are not here by accident, but for a divine purpose. God chose you for His lofty purposes. Again, I want to emphasize that, though over seven billion people inhabit this planet, not a single person is just like you. You are truly and divinely unique. God has counted the number of the hairs on your head, and you can be confident that His plans for you are wonderful (see **Isaiah 55:9**). His thoughts toward you are simply amazing (see **Psalm 40:5**). In fact, Scripture reveals that God's thoughts toward you are more numerous than all the grains of sand in the entire world:

> *My frame was not hidden from You when I was being formed in secret [and] intricately and curiously wrought [as if embroidered with various colors] in the depths of the*

earth [a region of darkness and mystery].
Your eyes saw my unformed substance, and
in Your book all the days [of my life] were
written before ever they took shape, when
as yet there was none of them. How
precious and weighty also are Your
thoughts to me, O God! How vast is the
sum of them! If I could count them, they
would be more in number than the sand.
When I awoke, [could I count to the end] I
would still be with You.

Psalms 139:15-18 AMP

Hopefully, by now you are convinced of your
value in God's eyes and the positive impact that
He has created you to have on your own life and
on the lives of many others. Later in this book, I
will discuss how to release blessings and
protection upon your family and your descendants.
The power of proclamation is enormous! You have
been given an outstanding sphere and scope of
authority with people, especially your bloodline.
My goal is to teach you to use that authority and
help you learn how to speak and release divine
blessings and break family line curses.

Now let me explain what I am referring to
when I use the words *lineage-line.*

"I am the God of your father Abraham; do not fear for I am with you. I will bless you and multiply your descendants for My servant Abraham's sake."
Genesis 26:24

CHAPTER 2
What Is Lineage-Line?
Is It Important?

The Word of God has much to say concerning the value of lineage or generational lines (see **Matt. 1:1-17; Luke 3:23-38**). Throughout the Old Testament, God continually identified Himself as a generational God, stating, "I am the God of Abraham, Isaac and Jacob" (see **Exod. 3:6**).

In **Genesis 26:24**, when the Lord appeared to Isaac, He said, *"I am the God of your father Abraham; do not fear for I am with you. I will bless you and multiply your descendants for My servant Abraham's sake."* And in **Deuteronomy 7:9**, we see the promise that blessing will flow from one generation to another:

Therefore know that the Lord your God, He is God, the faithful God who keeps covenant and mercy for a thousand generations with those who love Him and keep His commandments.

This wonderful promise motivates us to set high standards of conduct. If we seek to please God and honor Him with our lives, He will keep His promises to us likewise the generations that follow us.

Conversely, in **Deuteronomy 5:9-10**, a powerful warning is released concerning the damage one generation can bring upon another by its lack of love and loyalty to God. Speaking to Israel about idols, God said,

You shall not bow down to them nor serve them. For I, the Lord your God, am a jealous God, visiting the iniquity of the fathers upon the children to the third and fourth generations of those who hate Me, but showing mercy to thousands, to those who love Me and keep My commandments.

If we fail to obey God and His holy Word or if we live a life without regard or respect for God, the result will be an evil lifestyle being passed down upon coming generations. On the other hand, the promise of God's mighty grace and overflowing favor and blessing is to the thousandth generation for those who choose to love and yield to Him.

Walking in obedience to the Word and will of God produces lasting fruit that will be enjoyed by many generations.

This promise is in force today, just as it was in the day when it was spoken:

> *You shall therefore keep His statutes and His commandments which I command you today, that it may go well with you and with your children after you, and that you may prolong your days in the land which the Lord your God is giving you for all time.*
>
> ### *Deut. 4:40*

As we seek first the Kingdom of God, we are promised wonderful mercies and goodness—for us, for our children, and for their children as well (see **Matt. 6:33**).

We must make up our minds to put God first in our lives and remove anything that comes between Him and us. The blessing and benefits of such actions will be great—for us as well as for our children and grandchildren (see **Psalm 145:1-8**).

LINEAGE-LINE AND LEGACY

Let this be a time of a fresh start again I want to encourage you it is never too late. God is a God of love and mercy and He can turn things around.

Get ready to experience a fresh start.

And we know that all things work together for good to those who love God, to those who are the called according to His purpose.

Romans 8:28

CHAPTER 3

Fresh Start

God Brings About Beauty From Ashes

Scripture clearly warns us that the devil comes to steal, to kill, and to destroy. Yet Jesus Christ said that He had come so that we might have life that is overflowing and happy.

> *The thief does not come except to steal, and to kill, and to destroy. I have come that they may have life, and that they may have it more abundantly.*
>
> *John 10:10*

Christ Jesus has the power to turn any life around and to bring beauty from ashes.

> *To console those who mourn in Zion, To give them beauty for ashes, The oil of joy for mourning, The garment of praise for the spirit of heaviness; That they may be*

called trees of righteousness, The planting of the Lord, that He may be glorified."
Isaiah 61:3

No matter how difficult our lives have been or are even now at this moment, our God is able to restore and to turn events around.

Therefore, if anyone is in Christ, he is a new creation; old things have passed away; behold, all things have become new.
2 Corinthians 5:17

All we need to do is ask God for a fresh, clean start, and receive His awesome offer of grace.

Create in me a clean heart, O God, And renew a steadfast spirit within me.
Psalms 51:10

We must never forget that what the devil means for devastation, God has a way of turning for good. Through Christ's redemptive blood, He can turn the terrible and tragic events of our lives into His triumph, resulting in lives of victory.

And we know that all things work together for good to those who love God, to those who are the called according to His purpose.

Romans 8:28

My Personal Experience

My own life provides a vivid example of how a person's life and lifestyle affects others. My father, who I never actually saw, died at the age of thirty-seven, not long after I was born. My father stood over six feet and five inches tall and was a strong, handsome man. He had an excellent job, operating heavy equipment and building highways all across our nation. However, he began to engage in a lustful lifestyle and to have sexual encounters with various women. His playboy behavior would carry a high price tag, and he would soon learn that there is a high cost for low living.

As a pastor for over twenty-six years and a minister for over four decades, I have dealt with numerous people who live much like he was. When confronted, they excuse themselves, saying, "I am not hurting anyone but myself! What I do is my own business!" This is a huge lie. What we do has lasting effects on us and on our descendants. In my case, my father's sinful lifestyle almost cost me my life, even before I had lived a single day.

LINEAGE-LINE AND LEGACY

My dear mother found herself in a terrible situation because of the actions of my father. Mother had given birth to two children—first my sister, Kay, and then, a year later, my brother, Glenn. Now she was pregnant with me, but my father was extremely sick with a sexually transmitted disease that would ultimately take his mind and his life. In the midst of this, the doctors talked with my mother, informing her that the baby within her body would be afflicted with the same disease that was killing his father.

It was 1943, and my mother was extremely desperate! Not wanting to see an innocent baby destroyed by this horrible disease, she took a coat hanger, turned it into a hook, and inserted it into her body, attempting to extract my life.

I can't explain what happened next in natural terms because it was supernatural. When my mother tried to abort me, Christ Jesus literally covered me with His hand while I was in my mother's womb and kept her from destroying my life. Never doubt that God has power to bring about His plans. In Jeremiah 1:4 we see that God does have a plan, and He can select a person to accomplish a particular deed even before that person's birth.

When I was growing up in the sand hills of East Texas, times were incredibly difficult for our family. By the time I was less than a year old, my father had died in a mental institution as the result of his sexually transmitted disease. His death was dreadfully agonizing; slowly, the disease had ravaged his mind until he did not recognize his wife or his two children. Truly, there is a *high* cost for *low* living.

My dear mother was attempting to raise three children with no husband and almost no money. She took in as much washing and ironing as she could just to put food on the table. We were dirt poor in the truest sense of the phrase; however, we deeply loved each other and enjoyed being together. My two siblings and I were "stair-step" children. I was the youngest. My brother, Glenn, was one year older than me, and Kay, my sister, was two years older than me.

Adding to the difficulty of those years was the fact that Glenn had been born with crumbling of the hipbones and was crippled, unable to walk without crutches. I still have very vivid memories of pulling him around in a red wagon. It seemed that Glenn's only hope of ever walking would be through medical help that our mother simply could not afford. All this was the setting for a very significant moment in my young life.

God is good, and even when we are distant from Him; His plans for us are in progress. One day, when I was around four years old, I was outside playing when I heard an extremely clear voice in my head say, *"Don't get on that pony!"*

I didn't know anything about a pony, and I also didn't know anything about the voice in my head, so I asked out loud, "What pony?"

Suddenly, I felt like my entire body had been shocked with electricity that froze me in my tracks. I heard the voice again, not in my head this time, but right in front of me. It was an audible voice that I heard with my ears, ***"Don't get on that pony!"***

The moment I was able to move again, I ran into the house, into my room, and I jumped into my bed. My brother said, "What's wrong with you?"

"Don't get on that pony!" I replied.

"What pony?" Glenn asked.

I said, "I don't know; just don't get on that

pony!" For the next several days, every time I got quiet and still, the same voice would speak to me, reminding me not to get on the pony.

A few days later, Mother put some of my and Glenn's clothes in a box and fixed up a picnic lunch. My uncle arrived in a big, shiny car and opened the trunk, and Mother put the box of clothes in. Then Glenn and I climbed into the back seat, Mother got in the front with our uncle, and off we drove. As a four-year-old boy, I was excited to sit in the back seat of this big, new car and watch as we drove through one small town after another.

At one point, we even stopped at a distant roadside park and ate our picnic lunch. I was extremely excited to be going on a trip, but even as young as I was, I couldn't help but notice that my mother did not seem very happy. I could see a shadow across her heart and a troubled look in her eyes.

After countless hours of driving, we finally pulled up in front of a large ranch house. As our uncle parked the car, Glenn and I strained our necks to see what was going on and where we were. Suddenly, from around the corner of the big building came a woman leading a small pony. She was carrying two cowboy hats and toy pistols. My uncle opened our car door as the woman approached. The first words out of her mouth were, "Hello, boys. Get on the pony, and let's take a ride!"

My eyes grew wide from shock, and I slid all the way over to the other side of the seat next to Glenn, and we both started screaming, "I ain't getting on that pony! I ain't getting on that pony!"

That's when our mother began crying and said, "I just can't do it. I will not do it." She told our uncle, "Turn this car around and take us home."

Later I learned that they had taken us to an orphanage that eased the separation of children from their families by distracting them with a pony ride. But God had intervened and saved Glenn and me from separation from our family. Psalm 25:9 confirms that God guides and directs the humble and instructs them in His ways of justice. How I praise God today for speaking to a little boy with a strong warning that helped keep a struggling family together! God is so good!

Nahum 1:7 says, *"The Lord is good, a stronghold in the day of trouble..."* Let our souls rejoice over the promise of divine protection released in **Psalm 46:1**: *"God is our refuge and* *strength, a very present help in trouble.* " Truly, it will take an eternity to discover how wide, how long, how deep, and how high the love of God is for us!

The most important prerequisite to walking in victory is having hearts that are receiving an ever-increasing understanding of God's unfathomable love. Nothing we can do will ever stop *Him* from loving us. We should never doubt that God's plans and purposes for each of us are high and lofty (see **Jer. 31:17**), that His ways are wonderful and much higher than we could choose for ourselves (see **Isa. 55:9**). Through the ministry of the Spirit of revelation in our hearts, we must grasp the extent of God's abounding grace and lovingkindness toward us. His consuming passion and tender mercies will assure us of victory. And because we know that victory is His heart's desire for us, we can have boldness and the courage to overcome all obstacles.

If God went to such lengths to keep a dirt-poor Texan family together, you can be certain that cares about you and your situation, whatever it may be. If He worked in my family to bring us victory over all the obstacles and circumstances that threatened to pull us apart, He will also help you to walk in victory all the days of your life.

Even when we don't see it in the moment—because of our pain and problems—God is working in our lives to produce grace so that our good will come to pass (see **Rom. 8:28**). When we grab onto that grace and live victorious lives, we will be a blessing to ourselves and to our children. I cannot say it too much. God has a good plan for each of us, and His ways are always higher than our ways. The love of God knows no limits, and His grace and tender mercies reach deeper than our pain and sin. He is the one initiating this love affair. *"We love Him because He first loved us"* **(1 John 4:19**).

Blessed (happy, fortunate, to be envied) is the man who fears (reveres and worships) the Lord, who delights greatly in His commandments (AMP).
Psalm 112:1

CHAPTER 4

Goals and Guidelines for a Successful Life

The Influence and Inspiration of a Godly Life Is Priceless; Godly Reverence Produces Great Fruit

The goals and guidelines for a godly life are revealed very clearly in Psalm 112. One of the most valuable attributes we can instill in our children is a wholesome reverence for God. The pathway to a victorious, successful life is love, reverence, and respect for God. Here's what **Psalm 112:1** says:

> *Blessed (happy, fortunate, to be envied) is the man who fears (reveres and worships) the Lord, who delights greatly in His commandments (AMP).*

This exhortation to revere the Lord is addressed to all the people of God, and it is so essential for our day. We are to be people who love and honor the Lord, giving Him all of the glory, because we are His workmanship (see **Eph. 2:10**). Let's meditate on the overwhelming benefits of loving and fearing the Lord. The psalm uses the words *blessed, happy,* and *fortunate,* and the phrase *to be envied.* All of these describe the person who fears (or deeply reveres) and worships the Lord, the one who delights greatly in His commandments— which are encapsulated in the Word of God, the Holy Bible. If we obey the Word of God, the blessings of God will overtake us (see **Deut. 8:18**). If we take time to meditate upon the principals taught in God's Word, we are guaranteed success (see **Josh. 1:8**).

One aspect of reverence is obedience, and it is a key to walking in victory (see **1 Sam. 15:22**). Obey the Lord. It's that simple. Many ask the question, "Why do so many believers live in a state of bondage and defeat?" One of the main reasons is the fact that they have left their first love (see **Rev. 2:4**). If we want to be happy and blessed, we need to swiftly and completely obey God. Our first prayer must be a prayer of confession and repentance, asking the Lord to reveal and remove all things that have separated us from true intimacy with Christ (see **1 John 1:9**). Seeking to repent and return to our first love must become our first priority. Our second prayer must be, "Lord, restore my passion for You!" Christ has provided for us overwhelming victory through His blood. Therefore, there is no need—or excuse—for us to continue living in defeat. Victory, however, will require our dedication to overcoming strongholds. As part of that, we must ask God to reveal anything in our hearts that is dark and deceptive (see **Ps. 139:23**). If we will reaffirm our faith and rededicate ourselves to radical obedience, we can leave defeat in the dust and start walking in lifelong victory.

We must never forget that we are called to be in union and complete fellowship with Christ. Therefore, we must ask the Holy Spirit to *extract* from our lives anything that *distracts* us from Christ moving in our lives. The wonderful old gospel hymn says it so well:

> *Trust and obey,*
>
> *For there's no other way*
>
> *To be happy in Jesus,*
>
> *But to trust and obey.*

One of the most important aspects of the Christian walk is learning to quickly obey the voice of the Spirit of God. Just hearing the Word (voice) of the Lord is not enough; doing what He says is what matters (see **James 1:22**). Obedience assures us victory in the long run, even if we experience setbacks and hardships at times. Victory will be ours because the Victorious One abides within us.

The word *obey* is one of the strongest words in human language for the concept of hearing. Obeying the voice of Jesus is the only true evidence that we have heard Him. If we do not obey, we might as well be deaf; the result is the same. In fact, lack of obedience is evidence of lack of faith. James said that faith without works is dead (see **James 2:26**), and Jesus warned, *"Not everyone who says to Me, Lord, Lord, shall enter the kingdom of heaven, but he who does the will of My Father in heaven"* (**Matt. 7:21**). True faith is always revealed in obedience, which is why the word in the New Testament that is usually translated as "faith" also means "faithfulness." Our faithfulness is measured by the degree of our obedience to our prime directive from Christ: *"But seek first the kingdom of God and His righteousness; and all these things shall be added to you"* (**Matt. 6:33**).

Sadly, many Christians have spent too much of their lives in disorientation and defeat because they simply have not obeyed the Word of God. Only as we seek first the Kingdom and righteousness of God—His priorities—will we receive clear guidance and revelation, not to mention provision for all of the practical necessities of life that the rest of the world sweats and labors and worries over.

One source of confusion for many believers is the fact that they try to walk in the light of their own sparks rather than in the light of God's revealed Word. They make vital decisions based on their own desires and other earthly, temporary matters instead of seeking first the purposes of God's Kingdom. If we will make all of our decisions out of the commitment to seek the purposes of His Kingdom first, everything else will be added to us—without struggle or stress. That's the force of the Lord's promise in Matthew 6:33. When we put obedience to His purposes first, we will have nothing to be anxious about, knowing *who* our source and protector is. Obedience is the key to everything, but we must obey the right things—the will and Word of God.

There is no greater freedom and no greater peace than that which results from living our lives dedicated to the Lord in all things. No matter what our past has been like, we must let our past stay in the past because God created us to be the head and not the tail. His plan is for us to be above and not below (see **Deut. 28:13**). Now is the time to walk in freedom, and freedom is found in obedience. Knowing that we are in the will of God—that we are living in obedience—will produce great peace in our hearts.

Keeping our focus on the will of God will bring confidence, because we will know that—whatever we are called to do—we are not alone in our task. He is with us all the way (see **Josh. 1:9**).

Righteous Living Produces Blessed Children

Great wisdom is released in Psalm 112, which reveals the benefits and blessings of living an upright Christian life. An outstanding promise is released for all who obey its directions. One way to release blessings and success upon ourselves, as well as our lineage-line, is through our words. Our words have power to heal and to release vision and destiny.

A verbal blessing is made up of three powerful influences: God's Word, God's name, and our words. The power of our words is affirmed by the Scripture that states, *"Death and life are in the power of the tongue...”* **(Prov. 18:21)**. With verbal blessings, the tongue has great potential for good, because a blessing can overcome a curse just as light is superior to darkness.

For this reason, we must take time to speak and declare the promises revealed in **Psalm 112:2**: *“His [spiritual] offspring shall be mighty upon earth; the generation of the upright shall be blessed”* **(AMP)**. First, **Psalm 112:2** promises, *“His seed shall be mighty upon earth...”* **(KJV)**. This is an outstanding promise that a godly and yielded life will greatly affect our children and our children's children. Successive generations of God-fearing men and women will come from our houses, and they will be strong and influential in society because they will have great authority.

The good God-seeds we plant within the lives of our children and grandchildren will bring a great harvest in days to come.

Aunt Alice's Pear Tree: Fruit for the Future

Aunt Alice, a dear precious saint in my first pastorate, Rock Hill Baptist Church in Brownsboro, Texas, gives us an example that illustrates my point perfectly. On a warm, wonderful spring day, I was driving about the community. As I approached Uncle Walter and Aunt Alice's home, I was shocked to see Aunt Alice—who was in her eighties—standing at the edge of her yard with a pick and shovel, working on digging a hole.

When I stopped to check on her, because of her age, I discovered that she was planting a small pear tree. I questioned her, reminding her that it would take years before her pear tree would bear fruit. She looked deep into my eyes, with a wonderful twinkle in her eyes and a bright smile, and she replied: "Oh! I am planting this tree for coming generations to enjoy!"

That day I discovered a truth about living for the benefit of the coming generation. Over forty years later, I drove down the lane where Uncle Walter and Aunt Alice had lived. I looked and, behold, there stood a huge, lovely, fruit-bearing pear tree. I stopped the car, walked to the tree, reached with my hand as high as I could, and plucked a delicious, juicy pear. Holding the fruit, my heart overflowed with the memories of a life well lived and the many hearts and lives this dear, simple, godly couple had touched and transformed for the Kingdom of God.

As a young couple, they would hook up horses to a wagon and drive about the community, picking up boys and girls to bring them to Sunday school and church. Uncle Walter would strum songs on an old banjo as the wagon loaded to overflowing with precious living cargo and clattered and jangled to the church for Sunday school and worship.

Today, great fruit remains in this community from their ministry—especially a thriving, flourishing church that is reaching souls for Christ and advancing the Kingdom of God. The many seeds of love and compassion sown by this dear couple are still today bearing much fruit.

I was so blessed when, driving down highway 31 in Brownsboro, Texas, I saw the beautiful sign declaring: THIS IS THE FUTURE HOME OF ROCK HILL BAPTIST CHURCH. Months later the news media was filled with stories of this brand new cutting edge mega church with several thousands attending resurrection Sunday.

Because of seed sown in previous generations, they have outgrown their buildings and are enlarging. Uncle Walter and Aunt Alice illustrated to us how to make preparation for the coming generations.

LINEAGE-LINE AND LEGACY

Not only will we be blessed, happy, fortunate, and envied when we live in obedience, but these verses also promise that our children and our children's children will be as well. God desires to pour out His overflowing blessing on us and our children (see **Isa. 44:3-4**).

Though righteous saints may be persecuted and mocked, they will not be forsaken; the curses of people cannot deprive them of the blessing of God. Balaam's words were true: ***"...He has blessed, and I cannot reverse it"*** (**Num. 23:20**).

The children of the righteous also are under the special care of Heaven, and they shall inherit divine blessing. Thus, honesty and integrity are better cornerstones for an honorable house than mere wealth and materialism. The legacy of fearing God and walking uprightly is a higher nobility than blood or birth can bestow.

The gift of godly parents and grandparents is precious beyond words. We must expect that our children will be blessed and will prosper, quoting this promise over our families: ***"His [spiritual] offspring shall be mighty upon earth; the generation of the upright shall be blessed"*** (**Ps. 112:2**).

Abundance in Your House

The next verse in this psalm reads, ***"Prosperity and welfare are in his house, and his righteousness endures forever"* (Ps. 112:3 AMP).** This verse takes the promise of godly generational impact even farther; it reveals that ***"Wealth and riches shall be in his house..."* (KJV).** Material wealth is part of the spiritual blessing promised in this passage and throughout the Bible. In fact, Scripture states that it is God's plan to give us the ability to acquire wealth, not for our own purposes, but to establish His covenant:

> ***And you shall remember the Lord your God, for it is He who gives you power to get wealth, that He may establish His covenant which He swore to your fathers, as it is this day (Deut. 8:18).***

It is the will of God to bless His people, and we must not settle for less than what God has promised. Rather, we must contend for the blessing that belongs to us, as well as to our children and their children. **Ecclesiastes 5:19** states:

> ***As for every man to whom God has given riches and wealth, and given him power to***

eat of it, to receive his heritage and rejoice in his labor—this is the gift of God.

Honor and integrity are the road to favor and divine success; God promises that honest people will be blessed. Of course, we must remember that the blessing of God is more than just material wealth. Some things that God blesses us with are far more precious than gold and silver! Riches and worldly wealth can't produce a contented heart. In fact, I've met folks who had almost nothing, yet their lives were glowing with the grace and presence of God. The heart that is cheered with the favor of Heaven is truly rich beyond words. Scripture reminds us it is in God's Presence fullness of joy is found (see **Psalms 16:11**).

The second part of this verse promises that the righteous will stay their course, speaking of their steadfastness. The righteousness of a true saint endures forever because it springs from the same root as the righteousness of God and is, indeed, the reflection of it. Thus, the righteous will wax stronger and stronger, and they will possess stability, strength, and courage for changing times. We need not shudder in fear, but we can walk uprightly and with confidence, knowing that we are created for victory. As we walk in obedience, we can expect to be filled with the favor and strength of God.

Light in the Darkness

Verse 4 of this psalm continues: ***"Light arises in the darkness for the upright, gracious, compassionate, and just [who are in right standing with God]"* (Ps. 112:4 AMP).** The first part of this promise is, *"Unto the upright there arises light in the darkness..."* In other words, the Lord will bring us light in due season. Good people still sometimes face pain and problems, but they are called to endure the night season with hope. Scripture promises, when we do this, that even though weeping might last through the night, joy will come in the morning, and the dawn of a new day shall arise (see **Ps. 30:5**).

We must expect to walk in the wisdom and light of God's guidance. Let us thank and praise God that His tender mercies are new every morning; great is His faithfulness (see **Lam. 3:20-23**).

Walking in the Light or Stumbling in Darkness

We are indeed without an excuse because it is the will of God for us to clearly know His divine purpose and plan for our lives. Get ready! You are about to receive keys to help unlock Kingdom purpose for your life. We are a people of divine purpose; our generation has been given an open door to advance the Kingdom of God like none other before us. Thus, it is crucial for us to gain a much deeper understanding of our divine purpose. We must know *who* God is in order for us to know who He has destined us to become.

In the Book of Daniel, we discover the benefit of knowing God, which is the release of mighty power for divine purpose (see **Dan. 11:32**). God will never give us an assignment without releasing for us an anointing to accomplish the mission. Never will we receive a task without a corresponding touch of grace to see us through. God is working in us both to will, as well as work, His divine plan. As Scripture says, *"For it is God who works in you both to will and to do for His good pleasure"* (**Phil. 2:13**).

We are instructed and equipped to understand God's revealed will. None of us need to continue to stumble blindly in the dark; rather, we are called to walk confidently in the light (see **Eph. 5:14-18**).

In this book, I will give you keys from the Word of God that will aid you in walking in true fellowship with Christ. One key to living a life of faithfulness to Christ Jesus is to learn to obey Him in the smallest details of our lives. *Little things do matter a lot.* Most of us have made the commitment deep within our hearts to obey God in the big issues; however, it is the little foxes that creep into the fields of our lives to damage and destroy the precious fruit. It is imperative that we protect the vines as well as the fruit in order to have fruit that will remain (see **Song of Sol. 2:15**).

In this book, one of our goals is to become better equipped to eradicate these little foxes, thereby enabling us to take our place as bold, confident leaders in the Body of Christ. The truth of God's Word will become a strong weapon to war against these foes (see **Ephesians 6:16-17**). It is time to eliminate the lies and walk in the truth. As we walk in the revealed truth of God's Word, we will experience daily victory from the strongholds of sin (see **John 8:32**). It is time to know clearly who we are and what we have been called by God to be and do. When we do, the Holy Spirit will anoint us with power to walk in the commission needed to accomplish these tasks for the advancing of the Kingdom of God.

We must develop hearing ears and obedient hearts. One of the most written statements from the lips of our Lord was, *"He who has an ear, let him hear what the Spirit says to the churches"* (see **Rev. 2-3**). One outstanding problem that is plaguing many in the Body of Christ is a lack of confidence in the power of God's Holy Spirit to equip them to accomplish the will of God. Many are paralyzed by the fear of not knowing enough. This is holding many back from launching out to do anything for the Kingdom of God. Vance Havner, a wonderful old-time preacher, once said, "I did not understand all about the plan of salvation. Neither do I understand all about electricity, but I don't intend to sit in the dark until I do!" We need not sit idle—we must get busy doing what we know we should be doing. Now is the time to extend our hands and hearts to grasp the keys that will help us to walk in true fellowship with Christ. This type of union will release the power we need to accomplish what God has asked us to do.

In the next few pages, you are about to discover just how precious and special you are—you are truly one of a kind.

Keys to Living God's Master Plan

God has a divine design and a special plan for your life. As I said before, you are truly unique.

God created you, and you are one of a kind.

One key to living a life of fruitfulness is truly understanding that each one of us is so incredibly unique. Not another single human being on the entire earth is just like you. Ponder that point for just a moment. With well over seven billion people alive today, not a single individual is like you. That is mind-boggling!

Think about the fact that God wanted you to be just like you are, yet fully yielded to Him. You are truly exceptional and divinely distinct, and you can accomplish something that no other person on this earth can. God truly made you special. It is awesome to think that no one can do the things that you can do. Put your hand on your heart right now and make this bold proclamation "Wow! I am really something! There is no one else like ME!"

There is a special mission and purpose that can only be accomplished by your life yielded to the control of God's Holy Spirit. Now that is true individuality!

God, in His sovereign wisdom, has made you special. The knowledge that God wanted you exactly like you are, yet totally yielded to Him, will greatly affect your confidence. As you yield to the anointing of God's Holy Spirit in your life, you will be able to do something for the Kingdom of God that no one else on earth can accomplish. God delights in placing His unique anointing upon ordinary people and enabling them to accomplish outstanding exploits for His glory. It's a fact God uses ordinary folks to accomplish the extraordinary.

You might say, "Oh, I am just too unimportant for God to use me." This is one big lie that must be confronted. God desires to use everyday people, ordinary men and women just like you and me, to accomplish extraordinary things. In this way, when the supernatural is accomplished, God receives all of the praise and glory (see **1 Cor. 1:26**). Nowhere is this truth exhibited more plainly than in the Book of Acts.

Here we see that when God commissioned one of His greatest apostles—Paul, a major leader in the New Testament—He did not summon some well-known leader, but a humble righteous man named Ananias. The Scripture declares that he was a common disciple. Can you believe it? God called for Ananias, a common disciple. What an awesome display of God using ordinary people to accomplish extraordinary deeds (see **Acts 9:10-19**). As we read this account, we cannot help but sense the deep communion that Christ shared with

Ananias. We can feel the committed life of this disciple through his response, *"...Here I am, Lord"* (**Acts 9:10**). Volumes are spoken in Ananias' greeting. It is easy to see that his was a life spent waiting upon the Lord, ready to obey the wishes of the King.

Honesty and Integrity

We must never forget that we present a more lasting lesson with our life than with our lips; our walk must match our talk if people are going to truly be transformed. Our children learn much more by watching than just hearing. They will learn valuable life skills if we show them trustworthiness in our daily affairs. But if our lives do not match our lips, we are not going to impress them in a favorable manner. We must teach them, by example, that it is much better to suffer for the truth than to be rewarded for a lie. We must illustrate for them that it is good to be wise and wise to be good. Our strengths will be shown in the things we stand for; however, our weaknesses will be revealed in the things we fall for. Reputation is valuable, but character is priceless.

Psalm 112:5 says, *"It is well with the man who deals generously and lends, who conducts his affairs with justice"* (**AMP**). The King James translates this verse, *"A good man shows favor, and lends: he will guide his affairs with discretion."* Righteous people know how to wisely use the talents that God has committed to them. We should instill within our children a kind and generous heart, helping them see that it is important to always to help others. We must have true integrity as followers of Christ; character, uprightness, transparency, and honesty are both expected and essential. How easy it is for us to bring shame and reproach to Christ by our lack of uprightness. It is actually sad how dishonest many so-called Christians are.

When people are sincerely upright, they exercise great care in managing their businesses and lifestyles in a manner that enables them to remain respectable, honest, and upright. Good people should not only be upright, but should be so discreet that no one may have the slightest reason to suspect them of being otherwise.

We live in a day of slander and accusation. But both are extremely devilish and dangerous, and we must live above them. It is easy to have our reputations slandered and our lives misrepresented in this day of cyber-reporting with cell phone videos and YouTube. Now more than ever, we must make up our minds to live above reproach, seeking to please the Lord Jesus in all we say and do (see **Col. 1:9-10**).

Our goal is to obey the Lord in every way so that we don't disobey and bring reproach on Him or on ourselves. They conduct their affairs rather than allowing the affairs to rule them; their accounts are straight and clear, their plans are wisely laid, and their modes of operation are carefully selected. Christian people should be prudent, thrifty, economical, sensible, and Christ-like in all their actions. We must never get so busy attempting to make a living that we forget to make a life.

In this day of liberal leaders and loose morality, many often call such people "fools" for their Christianity, but these mockers will not find the righteous so "foolish" when they come to deal with them. *"The beginning of wisdom"* (**Ps. 111:10**) has made them wise; the guidance of Heaven has taught them to guide their affairs well. Everyone can see that the righteous are people of character and common sense, and the wisdom bestowed upon them makes them great business people.

The children of this world often are, in their generation, wiser than the children of light, but there is no reason why this should continue to be true. As followers of Christ, we should be the most creative and inspired people on the planet. The Creator of the entire universe dwells within us, and He will release to us and for us the wisdom needed to succeed.

We can expect prosperity, protection, favor, and companionship as we stand as righteous children of God.

Permanence and Stability

Psalm 112 continues, *"He will not be moved forever; the [uncompromisingly] righteous (the upright, in right standing with God) shall be in everlasting remembrance* **(Ps. 112:6 AMP).** To the righteous, God promises, *"He will not be moved forever...."* God has rooted and established the righteous so that neither people nor devils will sweep them from their place (see **Romans 8:37**). They are steadfast and stable, not easily shaken, but standing strong and straight in a crooked and perverse world and shining brighter and brighter (see **Isa. 60:1-4**). The prosperity of the righteous shall be permanent, unlike that of the wicked. Their reputation shall be bright and radiant from year to year because it is not a mere pretense. The longevity of a good name is priceless.

Our good names and luminous reputations, passed down to our families, will not be soon forgotten, and *"...the righteous shall be in everlasting remembrance."* Our lives are like the work of a master sculptor chiseling into stone; they will not be soon erased. The righteous are worth remembering; their actions are of such caliber that they record themselves. None of us likes the idea of being forgotten, and the only way to avoid it is to live an upright, God-honoring life. If we honor *Him,* He will honor us. As C.T. Studd wrote in his famous poem:

> *"Only one life, 'twill soon be passed,*
>
> *Only what's done for Christ will last."*

Unshakable, Fearless, and Steadfast

Psalm 112:7 says, ***"He shall not be afraid of evil tidings; his heart is firmly fixed, trusting (leaning on and being confident) in the Lord"*** **(AMP).** In this verse, God promises that the righteous ***"shall not be afraid of evil tidings..."*** They will not be shaken by bad news because their hearts are firmly fixed on the steadfast promises of God (see **Matt. 7:24**). Righteous people reject rumors and evil reports; instead, they have learned to cast all of their cares upon the Lord, resting everything in the hands of God (see **Ps. 31:24; and Ps. 55:22**).

The righteous have hearts that are *"fixed, trusting in the Lord."* They are neither fickle nor faint. Even when they are unsure and a bit confused, they are still fixed in heart. Though they may change their plans, they do not waiver on the purpose of their souls (see **Ps. 27:14**).

When our hearts are fixed in steadfast, rock-hard reliance upon God, a change in circumstances will not throw us into a tailspin of doubt and unbelief; faith will make us firm and steadfast so that, if things get perilous, we will remain quiet and patient, waiting for the salvation of God.

An Established Heart: Firm Faith Produces a Strong Foundation

The psalm continues, ***"His heart is established and steady, he will not be afraid while he waits to see his desire established upon his adversaries"*** **(Ps. 112:8 AMP).** The phrase, *"His heart is established,"* indicates that the righteous have a love for God that is so deep and true that their confidence in God is firm and unshakable. Their courage has a firm foundation that is supported by

Almighty God. They have become settled by experience and confirmed by years. They are not rolling stones, but pillars in the house of the Lord. They *"shall not be afraid,"* and they are ready to face any adversary because a holy heart produces a brave soul (see **Prov. 28:1-2**).

The last part of this verse is so powerful: *"...Until he sees his desire established upon his enemies."* All through the conflict, even until they seize the victory, the righteous are devoid of fear (see **Ps. 27:1-5**). When the battle wavers and the results seem doubtful, they nevertheless believe in God, and they quickly reject despair, choosing instead to remain steadfast in confidence (see **Heb. 10:35**).

The Grace of Giving

The next verse reads,

> **He has distributed freely [he has given to the poor and needy]; his righteousness (uprightness and right standing with God) endures forever; his horn shall be exalted in honor (Ps. 112:9 AMP).**

The first part of this verse addresses the fact that, as followers of Christ, we are to exhibit the grace of giving. What we get is not just for ourselves. We need to have the attitude of the little lad who was willing to share his meager fish and bread with Christ and the thousands in need (see **John 6:9**). As Christians, we must be willing to distribute what we have to those who most need it. We are to be God's helpful hands, reaching out to a hurting world. The river of God's love flows with streams of liberality to supply help for the needy.

As Christ said, *"Give and it will be given to you: good measure, pressed down, shaken together, and running over will be put into your bosom…"* **(Luke 6:38).** The bigger blessing is in giving, not in receiving.

Unfortunately, some Christians are great at gathering, but very slow at dispersing; they enjoy the blessedness of receiving, but seldom taste the greater joy of giving. Jesus said, *"It is more blessed to give than to receive"* **(Acts 20:35)**— perhaps they think the blessing of receiving is enough for them.

Part two of this verse promises that our righteousness will endure forever. Actions speak louder than words, and our liberality will confirm our righteousness, proving its reality and securing its permanence. The character of the righteous is not spasmodic, but sure. We need steadfastness in the Church.

When we have learned how to walk in righteousness, the third part of this verse says that our *"horn shall be exalted with honor."* God shall honor His righteous sons and daughters (see **Deut. 28:4).**

In summary, the qualities of God-fearing people are kindness, benevolence, and generosity; these are essential to the Christian character. Being strictly religious is not enough because God is love, and He has called us to love our neighbors as ourselves. By this all people will know that we are God's followers—if we love one another (see **John 13:33-35**). Remember, love never fails! Let us surrender to God's great love and renew our lives afresh, stepping into the greatest breakthrough (see **Rev. 2:11**).

The Contrast Between Good and Evil

Lastly, **Psalm 112:10** says,

The wicked man will see it, and be grieved and angered, he will gnash with his teeth and disappear [in despair]; the desire of

***the wicked shall perish and come to
nothing* (AMP).**

This final verse in this passage states very
forcibly the contrast between the righteous and the
ungodly, between the saint and the sinner. This
contrast makes the blessedness of the godly appear
all the more remarkable. God promises that *"the
wicked man shall see it, and be grieved..."* The
ungodly shall first see the godly example of the
saints, to their own condemnation, and then they
shall behold the confidence and happiness of the
godly, to the increase of their misery. Truly we are
to become a radiant city set high on a hill that
cannot and will not be hidden.

The children of wrath will be obliged to witness
the blessedness of the righteous, though the sight
will make them bitter and sick in their hearts. They
will fret and fume, lament and become angry, but
they will not be able to prevent it because God's
blessing is sure and powerful. This verse says they
will even gnash their teeth in anger. Because they
are extremely wrathful and exceedingly envious,
they would like to grind the righteous between
their teeth, but they cannot do that, so they grind
their teeth against each other instead. The devil is a
poor paymaster; however, our faithful God is good
and does good for His people (see **Nah. 1:7**).

About the wicked, God's promise is that they will *"melt away."* The heat of their hatefulness will melt them like wax, and their desires will perish. The wicked will not achieve their purposes, but rather they will die as disappointed and defeated people. By wickedness, they hoped to accomplish their goals, but that very wickedness will become their defeat. In contrast, the righteous shall endure forever, and their memory shall always be remembered, but the ungodly will only be remembered with contempt and utter disgust. How wide is the gulf that separates the righteous from the wicked—both in this world and the world to come! How different are the portions that the Lord allocates to them!

May God grant us hearts surrendered to Him in obedience and overflowing with praise for God's astounding goodness to all who yield their lives to Him! God's goodness does not just last a lifetime, but rather, for all eternity we will enjoy the Lord and His goodness.

There are those who speak rashly like the piercing of a sword. But the tongue of the wise brings healings. Truthful lips shall be established forever, but a lying tongue is credited but for a moment

Proverbs 12:18-19

CHAPTER 5
The Power of the Spoken Word
Healing in the Words of the Wise

One of the most powerful tools we have to help shape and forge lives is our tongue. Our words have awesome power. *"Death or life are in the power of the tongue, and they who indulge in it shall eat the fruit of it, for death or life"* (**Prov. 18:21**). Most of us have heard the childhood rhyme, "Sticks and stones may break my bones, but words cannot hurt me!" This little jingle contains huge lies. Words actually can hurt; they have the power to inflict deep and lasting wounds. As it says in Proverbs:

> *There are those who speak rashly like the piercing of a sword. But the tongue of the wise brings healings. Truthful lips shall be established forever, but a lying tongue is credited but for a moment.*
> #### *Prov. 12:18-19*

Observe in this passage the reality that our words can be used as a deadly weapon, a sword cutting to the heart that inflicts deep, unseen wounds that no medicine can heal. The last phrase releases a promise of healing and hope if we yield our mouths to God's grace in order to put His truth within our words.

Then we can become instruments of healing. In a different translation, we read; *"Rash language cuts and maims, but there is healing in the words of the wise; lies are here today, gone tomorrow."* Our goal and aim is to speak positive, uplifting words to all we come in contact with, especially our families. *"Anxiety in the heart of man causes depression. But a good word makes it glad!"* **Proverbs 12:25**

Words can mold and develop confidence and character in them. We must be very careful to watch our words. As it has been said, "A person who has to eat his words seldom asks for a second helping!"

If our words are powerful enough to hurt, they can also be used for help. Proverbs 16:24 says, *"Pleasant words are like a honeycomb, sweetness to the soul and health to the bones."* Our words of affirmation and love can help our children build strong character, knowing that they are loved and accepted. Even when we need to correct them, we must do it with love and care. In moments of anger and frustration, if we are not careful, we can sow seeds of hurt and inflict deep wounds that can take years to erase.

It is tragic when a person finds it easy to say "I am sorry," over and over again, yet never stops to bridle the tongue before spouting hurtful and hateful words. It is so much wiser to turn off the faucet than to continue to mop up the water. Here is some biblical wisdom on the subject:

He who guards his mouth and tongue keeps his soul from troubles (Prov. 21:23)

Kind words heal and help; cutting words wound and maim (Prov. 15:4 MSG).

A gentle tongue with its healing power is a tree of life… (Prov. 15:4 AMP).

We must look for the good in our children and seek every opportunity to build them up. Affirmation is a strong bridge within our children, building confidence and courage to face life's difficulties. Bragging on their accomplishments will encourage them to even try harder.

LINEAGE-LINE AND LEGACY

This is good policy, not just for the parent and child relationship, but between husbands and wives, as well. Kindness knows no barrier; love truly works in every situation (see **1 Cor. 13:13**). How long has it been since you have taken time to be loving and kind to your loved ones? When was the last time you intentionally sought to lift their loads, brighten their lives, or even do something unexpected that causes their hearts to be filled with joy? It's a huge mistake to become so busy seeking to make a living that we forget to have a life.

The goal of our lives concerning our words can be found in the following passage: *"Let the words of my mouth and the meditation of my heart be acceptable in Your sight, O Lord, my strength and my Redeemer"* (**Ps. 19:14**). Similarly, one of the most beautiful passages concerning our words is **Proverbs 25:11**: *"A word fitly spoken is like apples of gold in settings of silver."* In other words, your kind and gracious words will release beautiful blessings in the lives of your loved-ones.

Here is the Message translation of this passage: *"The right word at the right time is like a custom-made piece of jewelry. And a wise friend's timely reprimand is like a gold ring slipped on your finger." (Prov. 25:11-12 MSG)*

Likewise, Solomon wrote in Ecclesiastes:

The words of a wise person are gracious. The talk of a fool self-destructs—He starts out talking nonsense and ends up spouting insanity and evil. Fools talk way too much, chattering stuff they know nothing about (Eccles. 10:12-14 MSG).

Outstanding advice is also released in **Proverbs 21:23**, *"Watch your words and hold your tongue; you'll save yourself a lot of grief"* **(MSG).** It is wise to think before you speak, seeking to understand the results of your words.

A soft answer turns away wrath, but a harsh grievous word stirs up anger. The tongue of the wise utters knowledge rightly, but the mouth of fools pours forth foolishness (Proverbs 15:1-2).

It has been said, *"nothing is more frequently opened by mistake than the mouth!"* Here is a guideline—"Lord, fill my mouth with worthwhile stuff. And nudge me when I've said enough." As people grow wiser, they talk less and say more. Never forget a careless word may kindle strife. A cruel word may wreck a life. A timely word may level stress. But a loving word may heal and bless.

LINEAGE-LINE AND LEGACY

Ask God to give you wisdom to use your words for good, following the wise counsel of this passage:

A gentle response defuses anger, but a sharp tongue kindles a temper-fire. Knowledge flows like spring water from the wise; fools are leaky faucets, dripping nonsense (Prov. 15:1-2 MSG).

Here is another awesome verse that is a good guideline to speak over our families:

"The Lord bless you and keep you; the Lord make his face shine upon you and be gracious to you; the Lord turn his face toward you and give you peace." So they will put My name on the Israelites, and I will bless them (Num. 6:24-27).

God has faithfully promised in the last four words of verse 27, *"I will bless them."* He does not do this because we deserve it. God does not love us because of what we do. Jesus Christ paid the price for our sins, and God blesses us because He has chosen to bless us. His grace knows no limit. His love knows no measure. His compassion has no boundary. His tender mercies are renewed every morning (see **Lam. 3:21-22**). It is God's will to bless us (see **Jer. 29:11**). In Christ Jesus we as well as our families are created to live victorious lives; because of this, we can expect to be more than conquerors actually super overcomers (see **Rom. 8:37**).

Maintain an Attitude of Gratitude

It is important to remember that the source of any blessing is the Lord Jesus Christ and that a supernatural power is released when we bless and praise His holy name. **Psalm 66:1-2 says, *"Make a joyful shout to God, all the earth! Sing out the honor of His name; make His praise glorious."*** King Hezekiah wrote Psalms 66 after the final overthrow of the Assyrians and General Sennacherib. Massive armies had surrounded Jerusalem—threatening Hezekiah and the nation of Israel—but during the night, the Angel of God moved through the enemy camp, leaving 185,000 dead Assyrians. In the morning, Hezekiah peered over the walls and could not believe his eyes. The spirit of praise fell upon him, and he shouted to the people of Jerusalem from the wall, *"Make a joyful noise unto God all you lands..."* We all have much to give shouts of praise for. When God destroys the enemies who were going to destroy our city and enslave our sons, it is time to make a joyful noise unto the Lord!

Never forget to maintain an attitude of gratitude for all God has done and is doing. When God heals your body, restores your broken marriage, opens the windows of Heaven and blesses you financially, it is time to make a joyful noise unto the Lord (see **Ps. 34:1**). Be sure to also share with your lineage-line the testimonies of the overflowing blessings and goodness of God in your life (see **Ps. 145:4-7**). This plants seeds of confidence deep within the soil of their souls that will bring lasting fruit. Always give God the glory and praise for the blessings, exalting His holy name and pointing to Christ as the source and resource of all your blessings.

The Power and Authority of Christ's Name

The Bible says, in **Psalm 150:6**, *"Let everything that has breath praise the Lord..."* It's time for the people of God to quit complaining about how difficult life is and to instead make His praise glorious (see **Phil. 4:6-8**). Let's give Him the glory due *His* name. Everyone's name means something, but there is only one that is above all others. It is a precious name, a powerful name, a saving name, and an eternal name. That name is *Jesus*. Look at what Jesus said about the power of His own name:

Up to this time you have not asked a [single] thing in My Name [as presenting all that I AM]; but now ask and keep on asking and you will receive, so that your joy (gladness, delight) may be full and complete (John 16:24 AMP).

Scripture states the name of the Lord is a strong and mighty tower that we can run into and where we will be safe (see **Prov. 18:10**). For this reason, we honor His name. As good parents, we all want our children to live under the blessing of God. As **Mark 10:16** says, *"And He took them up in His arms, laid His hands on them, and blessed them."* For this reason, we need to meditate more on the value and worth of Christ name. Then we can teach our children to also glorify the name of Jesus.

First, we bless His name because it is above every name by accomplishment! He is the only child born of a living God and the only Savior of men (see **John 3:16**). He is our joy, our hope, and our salvation (see **John 14:6**). There is no salvation apart from *Him* (see **Acts 4:12**).

We must teach our children to answer a truthful *yes* to the following questions. *Do you know Him? Do you love Him? Do you serve Him?* When we honor His name, we love what He loves, we hate what He hates, and we serve Him with passion. The greatest legacy we can leave to our families is this foundation, which will give them the courage to shout an affirming *yes* to the crucial questions asked above.

Second, we bless His name because His name is above every name by position! **Ephesians 1:21** says,

> *God has exalted Him far above all principality, and power, and might, and dominion, and every name that is named, not only in this world, but in the world to come.*

His name is a precious name. As the Bible says in **Matthew 16:18,** *"...upon this rock I will build my church and the gates of hell shall not prevail against it."* He is precious for what He has done; we bless His name because His name is a saving name!

Great will be our reward as we truly grasp the blessing and benefits of speaking words of blessings.

"Bless those that persecute you; bless and do not curse."
Romans 12:14

CHAPTER 6
The Power and Purpose of the Blessing
Every Individual Needs What the Bible Calls "THE BLESSING!"

The blessing of the Lord—it makes [truly] rich, and He adds no sorrow with it, neither does toiling increase it (Proverbs 10:22 AMP).

In the following passage, notice the overwhelming promise concerning our actions influencing our children. When we are truly hungry and thirsting after the Lord, seeking to abide in His presence, even our children will flourish.

For I will pour water upon him who is thirsty and floods upon the dry ground I will pour My Spirit upon your offspring and My blessing upon your descendants.

And they shall spring up among the grass like willows or poplars by the watercourses (Isaiah 44:3-4 AMP).

Our actions and reactions have long ranging effects for good or evil, helping or hurting, up to and over a thousand generations (see **Exodus 34:7**).

Make up your mind that you are going to release God's blessing upon your descendants. Join in this prophetic proclamation and directive declaration released in **Joshua 24:15**:

And if it seems evil to you to serve the Lord, choose for yourselves this day whom you will serve, whether the gods which your fathers served that were on the other side of the River, or the gods of the Amorites, in whose land you dwell. But as for me and my house, we will serve the Lord" (AMP).

Something extremely powerful transpires in the spiritual realms when we boldly decree the Word of God over our lives. Make this clear daring decree, and speak it out bold and loud right now:

"But as for me and my house, we will serve the Lord."

It is beneficial that we grasp a deeper understanding of the word for bless or blessing. It's used more than four hundred times just in the Old Testament alone. God Himself is the One who instigated and established the principal of releasing the blessing.

Defining the Blessing!

Question: What is the blessing according to the Bible? What does the Bible mean by bless or blessing?

Answer: From the *secular* perspective, a blessing, according to *Merriam-Webster's Collegiate Dictionary,* is "the act or words of one that blesses," or "a thing conducive to happiness or welfare."

From the Scriptural perspective, several words are usually translated as "blessing" or "bless" in the Bible. The Hebrew word most often translated as *"bless"* is *barak*, which can mean to praise, congratulate, or salute, and is even used to mean a curse. Genesis 1:22 is the first occurrence—when God blessed the created sea creatures and birds and told them to be fruitful and multiply in the earth. Likewise, in Genesis 1:28, God gave the similar blessing to Adam and Eve. However, a very important statement was added—they were to exercise dominion over creation (see **Psalm 115:16**).

When God called Abram to go to the Promised Land (see **Genesis 12:1-3**), He promised to bless him, make his name great, and through him, bless all the families of the earth. The blessings here were obviously associated with happiness and welfare, both for Abram and others.

Again in Genesis 22:16-18, God blessed Abram and added that the blessing was due to his obedience to God's commands. God changed Abram's name from Abram to Abraham. It will be beneficial to briefly reconstruct from Genesis the circumstances leading to this change in names.

In the very beginning of His conversation with Abram, God said to him:

> *Then I will make you into a great nation, and I will bless you, and I will make your name great, so that you will exemplify divine blessing (Genesis 12:2 NET).*

Abram was seventy-five years old when God informed him that his descendants would be numerous (see **Genesis 13:16**). Can you imagine the shock that Abram must have felt? Due to his advancing age, Abram asked God how this could be when he continued to be childless, and did He mean that Eliezer of Damascus would be the heir for this to come true? (see **Genesis 15:2-3**). God enlightened Abram in Genesis 15:4 that a son would come from his own body and be the heir.

It is always a massive mistake when we attempt to work out the plans and purposes of God in our human power. This is evident in the actions of Sarai and Abram. Due to lack of faith in God's promise, Sarai did not have the patience to remain faithful and trust in God, but rather gave their slave girl, Hagar, to Abram (see **Genesis 16:2**).

Ishmael was born because Abraham and Sarah did not trust God to fulfill His promise that their descendants would be from both of them. Scripture states that there is a way which seems right to man. However, that way leads to defeat and death (see **Proverbs 14:12**).

Abram was eighty-six years old when Hagar gave birth to Ishmael (see **Genesis 16:16**). It appears there is no record in the Bible concerning the thirteen years of Abram's life following the birth of Ishmael. When Abraham reached ninety-nine years of age, God instructed Abraham to walk blameless before Him:

When Abram was 99 years old, the Lord appeared to him and said, *"I am the sovereign God. Walk before me and be blameless. Then I will confirm my covenant between me and you, and I will give you a multitude of descendants"* **(Genesis 17:1-2 NET).**

Here God's rebuke appeared to indicate that during those thirteen years, Abram did not completely walk before God, and as a result, his life had blame.

Looking at the word, *blame,* God is saying to live a life that is filled with integrity, truthfulness, without blemish, complete, full, perfect, sincere, sound, without spot, undefiled, upright, and whole. This life only can be accomplished by having faith in Christ Jesus (see **Galatians 2:20**).

Also notice that God reintroduced Himself as "God Almighty." God gave Abram a condition—to walk before Him blameless and only then would He "confirm" His covenant between Himself and Abram. Here we see that the earlier covenant was not valid for those thirteen years and God wanted to reconfirm the same again. So God renewed His covenant with Abram:

As for me, this is my covenant with you: You will be the father of a multitude of nations.

No longer will your name be Abram. Instead, your name will be Abraham because I will make you the father of a multitude of nations.

I will make you extremely fruitful. I will make nations of you, and kings will descend from you (Genesis 17:4-6 NET).

God of Increase

Note: that in **Genesis 12:2** there was only one great nation—whereas in **Genesis 17:4-5**, God spoke about multitudes of nations. Here, God changed the name of Abram to Abraham and Sarai to Sarah. In the change of their names, we see God's wonderful desire to bless and increase. So Abram (*Noble Father*) became Abraham (*Father of many*) and Sarai, (*Princess*) became Sarah (*Mother of Nations*).

What is the significance of changing their names? What does it symbolize? God is the God of abundance and increase. The relationship of this change dealt prophetically with the future coming of the Messiah and consequently to a multitude of nations coming to Christ the King (see **Eph. 2:15**)!

God was not the only One who pronounced blessings. When Rebekah left her family to become Isaac's wife (see **Genesis 24:60**), her family pronounced this blessing upon her by saying, *"May you increase to thousands upon thousands; may your offspring possess the cities of their enemies"* **(NIV).**

Also when Isaac was ready to die, he pronounced this blessing on his son, Jacob:

> *"May God give you of heaven's dew and of earth's richness— an abundance of grain and new wine.*
>
> *May nations serve you and peoples bow down to you. Be lord over your brothers, and may the sons of your mother bow down to you. May those who curse you be cursed and those who bless you be blessed" (Genesis 27:28-29).*

Another Hebrew word for blessing is *esher*, which is also translated as happiness. **Job 5:17** declares: *"Blessed is the one whom God corrects; so do not despise the discipline of the Almighty."*

This blessing is connected to the knowledge that God is at work to direct us in the right path. We need to grasp the fact that God's chastisement is actually a display of His love for us. An example would be like a parent disciplining a child for playing in a dangerous place such as the middle of the street. The parent is not attempting to hurt the child but to protect and train the little one.

Psalm 1:1-3 conveys that theme further when stating:

Blessed is the man who walks not in the counsel of the wicked, nor stands in the way of sinners, nor sits in the seat of scoffers; but his delight is in the law of the Lord, and on his law he meditates day and night.

He is like a tree planted by streams of water that yields its fruit in its season, and its leaf does not wither. In all that he does, he prospers **(ESV).**

The Old Testament is filled with passages concerning the blessing of the Lord. The Book of Psalms is packed with references about delightful blessings for those who love and fear the Lord God.

The happiest people I know are those who obey the Lord Jesus and live according to God's Word. It is in His wonderful presence joy and gladness are found. (see **Psalms 16:11**)

In the New Testament, two primary Greek words are translated as "blessing." *Makarios* carries the meaning of happiness that we just referenced.

The Beatitudes of Matthew 5 and Luke 6 describe the happy state of those who find their purpose and fulfillment in God.

As in the Psalms, the best life is available for those who love and fear God and order their lives according to His Word. **Romans 4:6-8** ties this happy blessing to those whose sins are forgiven, for they know their relationship to God has been restored.

Eulogeo focuses more on good words or the good report that others give of someone and also describes the blessing that we say over our food (see **Matthew 26:26**).

This word is where we get our English word "*eulogy*," in which we speak well of one who has passed away. **Ephesians 1:3** blesses God for all the blessings that He gives us in Christ. **1 Peter**

3:9 instructs us to even bless those who mistreat us, because we were called to receive a blessing from God.

As we weave all these threads together, we see a beautiful tapestry revealing God's goodness. Understand that a blessing is a statement of good will and happiness that is said about ourselves and another, as well as the condition that fulfills those good words.

God's original design in creation was for His creatures, including mankind, to experience peace, prosperity, and fulfillment (see **Jeremiah 29:11**). That design was ruined when sin entered the world.

This blessing can only be restored by faith in the finished work of Christ Jesus (see **Colossians 1:13**).

Statements of blessing are a request for God to restore His favor on others or a declaration of His inherent goodness (see **Psalms 84:11**). The ultimate blessing that God has given is the new life and forgiveness that comes through faith in His Son, Jesus Christ (see **2 Corinthians 5:17**).

The material blessings we enjoy every day are temporary, but the spiritual blessings available to us in Christ encompass both time and eternity, as well as material and immaterial things. As the Psalmist said:

> *"Blessed are those whose help is the God of Jacob, whose hope is in the LORD his God" (Psalm 146:5).*

The Blessing is when someone significant to you believes in you and blesses your life by pronouncing and declaring a Bible based blessing over you. Understand these are not empty vain words—these are Divine promises that are revealed in the Word of God. Every person needs that. God counts on His people to give it to those with whom we have influence.

In the Bible, people clearly understood the power of the blessing. The children would come to their fathers and the father would lay his hands upon them and speak loving, faith-filled words about their futures and destiny. The children yearned and longed for that blessing. Again, those were not empty, hollow words of flattery or vain babbling. Those were words that helped to shape and forge their destinies. They understood the power of those words. They recognized that those words had the ability to bring success, prosperity, health, and abundance into their future. Never forget that the power of death and life are in our words (see **Proverbs 18:21**).

A powerful revealing story is found in Genesis 48 regarding Joseph bringing his children to their grandfather. Joseph's father was Jacob who had his name changed to Israel at a dramatic wrestling match with an angel. Jacob told the angel that he would not let the angel go until the angel blessed him. The angel spoke words over Jacob and his entire future transformed (see **Genesis 32:24**).

Consequently, Jacob had an uncanny understanding about the power of words. Think about it! How many people would wrestle with an angel? But then, how many people would not let the angel go until the angel blessed them? Jacob grasped that this truly was a *Divine Encounter* and determined to make the most of the moment. That event is an example that should motivate us to earnestly contend for our blessing. Don't be passive and lax when it comes to contending for your blessing. It is time to seek the Lord with all your heart (see **Jeremiah 29:12-13**).

Jacob, now Israel in Genesis 48, had never seen Joseph's boys because Joseph lived in Egypt. Israel asked who the boys were. Pay close attention to the first thing that Israel (Jacob) said when he realized who those young men were. After learning their identity, he instantly desired to release a divine blessing upon them.

"They are the sons God has given me here," Joseph said to his father. Then Israel said, "Bring them to me so I may bless them" (Genesis 48:9).

You can sense the excitement in Israel's request when he said to bring the boys to him so he could speak into their futures. He knew the power of proclaiming words and releasing the verbal blessing. This was an enormous event. Israel laid his hands upon Joseph's children and blessed them. Here is a part of what he said:

"The Angel who has delivered me from all harm—may he bless these boys. May they be called by my name and the names of my fathers Abraham and Isaac, and may they increase greatly upon the earth (Genesis 48:16).

We too are called to remind and reveal to the coming generations the goodness and mercies of God, and to tell them about God's wonderful, magnificent deeds (see **Psalms 145:1-15**).

This Blessing Was So Desired

The "blessing" was so desired that sometimes the children would fight over it. They did not fight over money or the family business—they fought over the words of blessing from someone they loved and respected.

In Genesis 27, there is the sad saga concerning how Jacob (discussed previously) wanted the blessing so badly that he lied and tricked his father, Isaac, into giving it to him instead of his older brother, Esau. Isaac was very old and practically blind. One day Isaac told Esau to hunt, kill some game, prepare it, and bring it to him. Isaac would then give Esau the blessing.

Prepare me the kind of tasty food I like and bring it to me to eat, so that I may give you my blessing before I die (Genesis 27:4).

Jacob's mother and Isaac's wife, Rebekah, overheard Isaac's instructions to Esau. Rebekah loved Jacob more (which wasn't right). Favoritism is a breeding ground for jealousy and competition among siblings. Rebekah conceived a wicked scheme—a conspiracy contrived to deceive her husband. She told Jacob to kill some goats and they would trick Isaac into blessing Jacob instead.

Jacob said something that is very interesting to his mother.

"What if my father touches me? I would appear to be tricking him and would bring down a curse on myself rather than a blessing" (Genesis 27:12).

This is extremely powerful. Jacob said that his father had the power to bless him or curse him. Think about that! Our parents have the ability to bless our lives or curse our lives. *We, as parents, have the power to bless our children or curse our children with our words.* No matter if we realize it or not, our words affect our children's future either for good or for bad. The words we speak possess tremendous transforming power.

A Word Curse

Our words today carry the same power that Isaac's words carried then. It is extremely important for each of us to always encourage our children and bless them. We need to tell them they can accomplish anything. I've heard far too often of parents being negative. *"Why can't you hit the ball like someone else? Why can't you make better grades in school? How are you ever going to amount to anything?"* With our negative foul words, we curse their lives. Never believe the lie "sticks and stones may break my bones, but words can never hurt me."

I'll give a painful personal testimony. One of the chores that my first son had was to mow the lawn. As a young lad, he would work very hard to cut the grass in the sweltering heat in Texas. One day he had just finished mowing the lawn and was putting away the mower as I drove into the driveway. He had done a very good job on a big yard, and I only saw one small strip he had missed. Instead of bragging and encouraging him about the great job on all the rest, I scolded him concerning the small part. At that point, the Lord spoke to me and humbled my heart. He said, "Bobby, what if I just pointed out the mistakes in your life? How would you feel?" So after repenting to the Lord and my son, I realized we need to look for the good and not the bad in other people.

Don't misunderstand me. I am not saying we can't correct our children, but if all we do is say words that discourage and belittle, we will destroy the child's self image. We will open up a door for the enemy to bring destruction into their lives. I know people today that suffer from words their parents spoke over them as a child. Much healing could occur if we would take time to break the power of the hurtful words and simply speak words of healing and inspiration to our family.

Years ago, my grandfather, James Benjamin Owens, would say to the entire clan, *"If you can't say something good about someone; don't say anything at all!"* He truly practiced what he preached—never would he speak hurtful or negative things concerning others, and he would not allow anyone in his house to do it. He had a no tolerance policy against any form of gossip or backbiting.

In many cases, children get their ideas of what God is like from their parents and especially from the father. If they get the idea that God is mean, critical, and belittling, the child will grow up with a distorted view of God. But if we will display the love and encouragement of God, our children will see God in a healthy way.

Ask God to make you a living example of His love and light to your entire family. Be a conduit to help transfer God's love and grace to your family.

Children are not always perfect, but don't emphasize their imperfections. On the other hand, emphasize what they do well. Encourage them they can do anything they set their minds to do.

Tell them they are wonderful and smart. Tell them they are blessed! Tell them how proud you are of them. Do this to your grandchildren as well.

Keep an open door of communication with your children and grandchildren so they are free to discuss and talk about anything with you. As leaders in the family, we are in many ways setting the rudder of their lives with our words.

Some of you have children that are grown and maybe live a great distance away. Pick up the phone and tell them how proud you are of them and how much you love them. You will be amazed how that will add direction to their lives. Don't let another day go without doing this.

Remember your words can be like apples of gold in settings of silver, which speaks of your words as being graceful and beautiful (see **Proverbs 25:11**).

In the story revealed in **Genesis 27** concerning Jacob and Esau, Jacob put on Esau's clothes and some goat's hair on his hands and neck, and went to his dad. Isaac asked who it was and Jacob said it was Esau. It is never God's plan for anyone to deceive and use dishonesty to achieve anything—especially the favor and blessing of God.

Jacob said to his father, *"I am Esau your firstborn. I have done as you told me. Please sit up and eat some of my game so that you may give me your blessing"* (**Genesis 27:19**).

It is normal and natural for all children to want their parent's blessing. Jacob convinced Isaac that he was Esau and Isaac gave Jacob the blessing. Look at what he said.

> *"May God give you of heaven's dew and of earth's richness— an abundance of grain and new wine.*
>
> *"May nations serve you and peoples bow down to you. Be lord over your brothers, and may the sons of your mother bow down to you. May those who curse you be cursed and those who bless you be blessed." (Genesis 27:28-29)*

Notice that Jacob's father declared great things over Jacob. He spoke into his future. He spoke powerful, prophetic words that blessed Jacob's life.

Not long after that, Esau came back. When Isaac discovered that Jacob had deceived him, the Bible said that he began to shake violently and Esau wept. Isaac said something necessary for us to understand and pass on to our children. Note how the NLB says this:

> ***Isaac began to tremble noticeably. Isaac: "Then who is it who was just here with venison, and I have already eaten it and blessed him with irrevocable blessing?"***
>
> ***(Genesis 27:33 NLB)***

By now you understand that our words carry transformational power. Supernatural power is released for your children when you declare and pronounce a blessing upon them. Use your words to speak blessings over your descendants as well as others. Showing confidence in someone has outstanding power to change and adjust their entire outlook on life. Declare great things for the future of your children and your grandchildren.

Speak God's Blessing Over Yourself

It is difficult to pass on a blessing if you don't understand that you are blessed yourself. These insights will help you have a good pattern so that you can declare some good Godly proclamations over your life today. Some of you have had all sorts of negative things spoken over you. This will change right here right now. God wants to bless you today.

LINEAGE-LINE AND LEGACY

Open your heart right now and receive God's wonderful blessing today!

Proclamation and Declaration

With a humble heart and an accessible spirit, open your life to receive these blessings. It might seem awkward at first but don't be shy. Make this a time of proclamation and declarations for your destiny and the destiny of your descendants. Take time to quote them over your life now. Something so powerful and transformational occurs when we speak aloud the promises of God.

> I declare in the name of Christ Jesus, that I am blessed with God's wisdom, and I have God's clear direction for my life.

> I declare that I am blessed with creativity, with courage, with ability, and with abundance.

> I declare that I am blessed with a strong will, with self-control, and with self-discipline.

> I declare that my family and I are blessed with good faithful friends, with good health, and with faith, favor, and fulfillment in life.

I declare that I am blessed with success, with supernatural strength, with promotion, and with divine favor and divine protection.

I declare that I am blessed with an obedient, cheerful heart and with a positive outlook on life.

I declare that any curse or negative evil words that have ever been spoken over me and my family are broken in the name and authority of Jesus Christ.(see **Isaiah 54:17**)

I declare that I and my family are blessed in the city. We are blessed in the country. We are blessed when we go in. We are blessed when we go out.

I declare that everything I put my hands to do will prosper and succeed.

I declare that me and my entire family are blessed and highly favored by Almighty God.

If you receive the blessing, then shout out loud:

"THANK YOU LORD!"

LINEAGE-LINE AND LEGACY

It is good to declare these blessings each day over your life. By doing so, this will saturate the spirit realm with these positive words of faith, and your heart will began to embrace them and your life will began to reveal their truth.

> *The LORD said to Moses, "Tell Aaron and his sons, 'This is how you are to bless the Israelites. Say to them: "The LORD bless you and keep you."*
>
> *(Numbers 6:22-23).*

Notice the way that God said to bless others is to *SAY TO THEM.* We bless people with our words. A blessing is not a blessing until it is spoken. Something very powerful happens when we declare it (see **Job 22:28 AMP**).

What kind of words does God want us to say? Words of blessing and protection—words that release peace and the awareness of God's abiding presence.

> *"The LORD bless you and keep you; the LORD make his face shine upon you and be gracious to you; the LORD turn his face toward you and give you peace"*
>
> *(Numbers 6:24-26)*

Speak words of encouragement and victory—words that release confidence and faith. Declare God's goodness. Declare words of God's favor. Declare that God's face is smiling upon a person. Blessing is when we declare God's goodness upon people.

Take time to gather your family. Turn off the television, unplug from the phone, and tablet. Close the computer, and the benefits will be worth it. Husbands bless your wives and wives bless your husbands. Parents bless your children. Children take time in your own words to bless your mother and father.

Learn to speak this blessing over your own life and into your future. Remember that a blessing is not a blessing until it is spoken. Use your words to bless. Give the blessing to your children and grandchildren. Declare God's favor. It will help you experience a new life of victory and abundance that God has planned for you.

CHAPTER 7

Parents Function as the Priesthood of Their Families

Blessing Our Children in the Name of the Lord

God places the spiritual responsibility for the family upon the shoulders of the father and mother. The role models for our children should not be sports stars or singers or even preachers or coaches. Rather, it should be their parents. The future of our nation will not be determined by presidents or politicians, but instead by what parents teach or fail to teach their children. Therefore, we must bless our children in the name of the Lord Jesus, releasing the power of God into their lives with spoken blessings. Let us lay our hands on them and speak healing into their minds and bodies—speak confidence, success, love, joy, and peace in their lives. We can shape their lives through the power of the blessing! As parents, we are the priesthood of the home. We cannot change what we will not confront. If we don't take charge of our children's lives through the power of the blessing, satan will.

Consider the power of the parental blessing. As parents, we have the power to speak life or death into the lives of our children. If you call your sons and daughters names like "stupid," "idiot," or "dumbbell," you have placed a curse upon their ability and motivation to learn! The solution is simple. Repenting of these words erases their power. As Christians, we must realize that curses are very real, but that they can be broken. **Romans 12:14** says, ***"Bless those that persecute you; bless and do not curse."*** What is a curse? A curse is a negative supernatural power initiated by speech.

The occult realm knows the power of spoken word curses. Words spoken by someone in spiritual authority set in motion a force that will continue from generation to generation until it is supernaturally broken. Words have power, and power has effect. Positive words have the power to convey God's blessing, healing, joy, confidence, and peace. Negative words have the power to bring emotional, spiritual, and even physical death. Thankfully, in Jesus we have the power to cancel the effect of the negative words that have been spoken over our lives.

Step one is to bless those who curse us. When Jesus was on the cross, the last thing He did was to bless His tormentors. *"**Father, forgive them, for they do not know what they do**"* (**Luke 23:34**).

Step two is to admit that others have knowingly or unknowingly spoken curses over our lives. This could go all the way back to our childhood or years ago in our painful past. We must not let the pains of the past keep us from the victories of the future. Instead, we must deal with issues now. Likewise, when we recognize that we have been the one placing the spoken word curses over others, we must repent and ask God to remove the words we have spoken.

Then, we should quickly replace those words with blessings. For example, imagine that, in a moment of anger or hurt or disappointment, I lashed out against my son, saying, "You are just dumb and stupid; you can't learn anything!" When I realize what I have done, I must repent and say, "I thank God for my son, who is bright and brilliant and able to grasp and learn all things." Just this simple repenting and restating will do wonders in the spirit realm. It will bind up forces of evil that were set in motion to damage our children, and it will release divine help to guide and instruct our children.

Step three is to identify the nature of the curse. Then, finally, we must pray aloud by name for each curse to be broken. "Father, in Jesus' name, I ask You to break the curse over me [and verbally name it]. I renounce it in the name of Jesus. I am free!" Scripture states that those whom the Son sets free are free indeed (see **John 8:36**). As children of God, we are entitled to His supernatural blessing. The blessing is the act of releasing the supernatural power of God into another person's life by the spoken word of spiritual authority. We must not live another day without the blessing of the Lord upon us and our families.

I've known families that caught the importance of receiving family blessings, and they travelled great distances to get the family blessing. As a leader of your family you owe it to your children to get together and lay your hands upon your offspring and pass along to them the spoken blessing. This will help them enter deeper into their destiny.

We are to bless those who love us as well as those who dislike us. In three New Testament books, God gives us direct instruction to bless those who curse and revile us (see **Matt. 5:44; Luke 6:28; Rom. 12:14**). Obeying this instruction produces results that are not expected by the one who gave the curse or the one who was cursed.

Throughout Scripture, the importance of verbal blessings is expressed numerous times. As parents, we can help mold and direct our children and even inspire them to achieve greater things in life by speaking verbal blessings. By blessing the child, the parents will be greatly helped in overcoming any disappointment, anger, or frustration, and the act of blessing will help instill a spirit of patience confidence, and love in the parents.

You might ask, "How do I bless my children?" The blessing should emphasize God's love for your children and His great purposes for them. Take time to show them the promises revealed in God's Word related to blessing because this will give them a firm foundation.

Let's look deeper into the promise and power of the spoken blessing. The blessing is the impartation of the supernatural power of God into a human life by the spoken Word of God's delegated authority. It is God's will to bless every aspect of our lives because we are created for victory.

When releasing a blessing, it is important to say aloud the promise. Speaking the blessing aloud somehow releases Heaven's help to perform it. Thus, supernatural blessing is invoked by speaking it aloud. Once the blessing has been spoken, it cannot be withdrawn! Only God can stop it because of the individual's disobedience, but no other person can stop it. Because of this power, once a spiritual authority speaks the blessing, we should fully expect God's great favor and blessing in our lives and the lives of our children (see **Job 22:28**).

Don't let the world around you squeeze you into its own mold, but let God re-mold your minds from within, so that you may prove in practice that the plan of God for you is good, meets all his demands and moves toward the goal of true maturity

Romans 12: 2 (Phillips)

CHAPTER 8

Guide Your Family's Discovery of Divine Destiny

Instill Faith Within Your Family, Helping All to See Their Value and Worth

One evening, as I pulled into the parking lot of the church where I was to speak, I noticed a bunch of young people gathered in a group outside the building. They were vivacious, laughing, jumping around, and having a great time together, as teenagers tend to do. Their lively spirit was very appealing, and I immediately felt drawn to them. I wanted to go over and talk with them and join in with their fun for a little while. However I noticed, off to the side, another teenager, a young lady who was by herself. Somewhat overweight and wearing thick glasses, she looked very despondent and obviously did not feel like she was part of the group. All at once, my intention to join the cluster of kids was arrested when I heard the Lord say to me, "Go over and speak to her." I did not know what He wanted to say to her; however, I could feel His compassion for her.

So I walked over to her, and as I approached, the Lord gave me a prophetic word for her. I said to her, "Honey, God is going to give you the power and ability to write a book." Just for a moment, her eyes lit up and a great ray of hope spread across her face. Then, even as I watched, doubt, like a dark cloud, covered her face again, and she looked just as despondent as before.

Several months later, I returned to that same church, and that same young lady met me at the front with her mother. She was elated and had in her hand a letter from the governor of the state, along with a newspaper article reporting that she had won first place in the state for a short story she had written and submitted. Now she was an integral part of the youth group, writing plays, skits, and scripts for them to perform. She was starting to come into her own.

By the standards of the world (and unfortunately, of far too many churches and youth groups), she was not one of the "beautiful people," but she was beautiful to God. Where some people might have seen a "plain Jane," God saw a precious jewel with a bright and promising future. And He told her so. In a few short months, she had changed from a "nobody" (in her own eyes) to a "somebody" with purpose and destiny. In God's eyes, of course, she had always been a "somebody"—she just didn't know it, until that day when, through me, God spoke a word to her that opened her eyes to who she really was.

This young lady's dilemma is not unique and is not limited to young people. Many today suffer from identity crisis. Saints of all ages struggle daily with their spiritual identity. They are as mixed up as a termite in a yo-yo, tossed to and fro with no idea who they are in Christ and little or no scriptural knowledge to give them a solid foundation. Such ignorance in a child of God is not only tragic, but also dangerous. God said, *"My people are destroyed for lack of knowledge"* **(Hos. 4:6a).** The apostle Peter warned us to, *"Be sober, be vigilant; because your adversary the devil walks about like a roaring lion, seeking whom he may devour. Resist him, steadfast in the faith..."* **(1 Pet. 5:8-9a).** Satan loves to pounce on immature believers who lack knowledge because, if he can keep them in the dark as to who they really are, he can prevent them from fulfilling their divine destiny.

God is not the author of confusion (see **1 Cor. 14:33**). He desires for us to know His plans and purposes for our lives (see **Eph. 5:14-18**). Satan, the accuser of the brethren and the mortal enemy of our souls, is a thief and a liar who is always busy seeking to rob believers of their true identity in Christ. Ignorance leads to bondage, while the road to freedom is paved with truth.

Jesus said, ***"You shall know the truth and the truth shall make you free"*** **(John 8:32).** The first truth we need to know is the truth of who Christ is. Second, we need to know who we are in Christ.

Heaven and hell are posing the same question to every person in the Body of Christ. The Spirit of God and the devil alike are asking us, "Who do you think you are?" It is an apt question, and the eternal destiny of millions rides on the answer. Without question, the Body of Christ today is in an identity crisis of unprecedented proportions. If we are to fulfill our spiritual destiny, we first must know who we are.

But before we can discover who we are, we must comprehend who Christ is, because it is only in relation to Him that we can understand our true spiritual identity. God created us in His image (see **Gen. 1:27**), and He has *"predestined"* all believers *"to be conformed to the image of His Son"* **(Rom. 8:29)**. What is the image of His Son, Jesus Christ? Paul gives us the answer: *"He is the image of the invisible God, the firstborn over all creation"* **(Col. 1:15)**, in whom *"dwells all the fullness of the Godhead bodily"* **(Col. 2:9).** And God wants to make us just like Him!

Even though we each are made in God's image, He also made each of us unique. God delights to display Himself in our individuality. He loves diversity! Every leaf on every tree is different from every other leaf. Every snowflake is different from every other snowflake. God even gave each of us our own personal and absolutely unique set of fingerprints.

There is no one else in the entire world like you. You are one of a kind by divine design. God created you to be uniquely you, and He endowed you with particular gifts, talents, and abilities so that you can fill your unique place in His plan and fulfill your destiny in life. No one else can do what God has called and equipped you to do—no one. Someone once said, "God don't make no junk." I have news for you: God don't make no clones, either! There are no copies of you anywhere in the world, and that's just the way God wants it.

The world hates nonconformists. It will try to shape us into its own cookie-cutter pattern so that we look and sound and act like everybody else. We must not let that happen! We are too precious to God and too important to the Body of Christ to allow our uniqueness to be squeezed out. Paul said, ***"Do not be conformed to this world, but be transformed by the renewing of your mind, that you may prove what is that good and acceptable and perfect will of God"*** **(Rom. 12:2).** One modern English paraphrase of this verse really gets the idea across:

> ***Don't let the world around you squeeze you into its own mold, but let God re-mold your minds from within, so that you may prove in practice that the plan of God for you is good, meets all his demands and moves toward the goal of true maturity (Rom. 12:2 Phillips).***

Rejoice in who you are—the person God made you—and don't worry about trying to be somebody you were not created to be. Somebody might be saying, "That may be fine for you, but I'm not an eloquent preacher or a talented musician. I can't teach, and I'm shy around people I don't know. I'm nobody special." God disagrees! The world may look at you that way, but God judges by a different standard. While the world pursues "superstars and celebrities," God searches for people who are hungry for Him, ordinary folk through whom He can do extraordinary things. It's time for you to except yourself, and realize you are precious and special to God.

Where the world judges by external appearances, God looks at the heart (see **1 Sam. 16:7**). So if your heart is right, if you are hungry for God, He not only can use you, but He wants to use you! However, it won't happen unless you believe it. Until you stop listening to what the world says about you and start listening to what God says about you, you will never realize your full identity in Christ or fulfill the destiny God has for you (see **Ps. 139:15-18**).

It all boils down to how we think, the attitude of our mind. The mind is where the battle for our destinies is fought. That is why Paul insists that we must have our minds renewed, which calls for a complete transformation of our thinking. We must learn to lay aside the worldly mindset and take up the "mind of Christ" (see **1 Cor. 2:16**). It's time to let the Holy Spirit purge us from our "*stinking thinking*" and receive the mind of Christ. Then we will be able to understand more clearly God's call and destiny for our lives.

One definition of *destiny* is, "the inner purpose of a life that can be discovered and realized." Discovering our divine destiny and realizing (accomplishing) what God has called us to achieve is the most important thing we can ever do. It's what we were born for. Renewing our minds, transforming our thinking from the world's point of view to God's perspective, will enable us to fulfill our destinies. Having renewed minds will aid us in carrying out Paul's instructions to *"put on the new man who is renewed in knowledge according to the image of Him who created him"* **(Col. 3:10).**

When we received Christ as our personal Savior, a great spiritual transaction took place: We received brand new hearts. At the moment of our conversion, God placed within us changed hearts, transformed hearts that made us capable of fully following His will. God promised through the prophet Ezekiel, *"I will give you a new heart and put a new spirit within you; I will take the heart of stone out of your flesh and give you a heart of flesh"* **(Ezek. 36:26).** A heart of stone is a dead heart, but a heart of flesh is vibrant with life. As Proverbs 4:23 states, *"Keep your heart with all diligence, for out of it spring the issues of life."* In other words, as our hearts go, so go our destinies. We can't fulfill our destinies until we know who we are, and in order to know who we are, we have to have our heads on straight.

God's Way Up Is Down

Beside the fact that God gives grace to the humble, another motivating factor for walking in true humility is that it is the steppingstone for launching us into deeper revelation.

Genuinely humble people receive wisdom and insight from God that is withheld from those who are proud, arrogant, or wise in their own eyes.

Such honor shown to the humble made Jesus rejoice:

> ***At that time Jesus answered and said, "I thank You, Father, Lord of Heaven and earth, that You have hidden these things from the wise and prudent and have revealed them to babes" (Matt. 11:25).***

The word *babes* here has nothing to do with chronological age, but refers to spiritual attitude and maturity. God resists the proud, but pours out His grace and favor on all who approach Him with the openhearted faith of a child. They are the ones to whom God reveals His greatest secrets.

Actually, God calls ordinary people and anoints them with an extraordinary anointing to accomplish outstanding displays of His power. He does this so that He will be the one who receives the glory. When people see amazing God-like things taking place in and through the lives of "ordinary" folk, they will know that God is at work, and they will glorify Him.

This is why the Bible does not have any "superstar saints." In the case of every Bible hero—*every one*—God took ordinary "nobodies" and did extraordinary things in and through them. Here are the two things that made them great: (1) the powerful anointing and presence of God on their lives and (2) their humble and obedient response to God through childlike faith.

Notice that we are to be *childlike*, not *childish*. I am not talking about immaturity here, but rather a tender heart and a gentle, humble, and teachable spirit. Some of the most powerful expressions of faith today are coming from small children. I am continually amazed at the overwhelming presence of Christ being manifested in the lives of children around the world. Many of them even are moving in awesome miracles and signs and wonders. I see it everywhere I go. Like children, we must come trusting totally in the faithfulness of our heavenly

Father, confident that He desires better for us than we could ever desire for ourselves. God loves us and always has our very best interests in mind. He said so Himself: ***"'For I know the thoughts that I think toward you,' says the Lord, 'thoughts of peace and not of evil, to give you a future and a hope'"*** **(Jer. 29:11).** Isn't it overwhelming to know that God thinks about us—that He thinks about each one of us personally—and that His thoughts toward us are thoughts of peace, hope, and a bright future?

God cares about every step we take and everything we do. He cares deeply about our every hurt, fear, joy, and sorrow. He cares about our dreams because He gave them to us and wants to see us realize them. One day God spoke these very encouraging words to me: "My people are about to believe what they know." The Spirit of God is going to move the Word of God from our heads to our hearts and to our hands. We will become doers of the Word and not just hearers (see **James 1:22**).

With this in mind, it is high time for us to let go and let the Holy Spirit have total control of our lives! We need not worry about letting go. God has more power to direct our lives than the devil does to deceive us. As John assures us, ***"You are of God, little children, and have overcome them,*** *because He who is in you is greater than he who is in the world"* (1 John 4:4).

The word *them* in this verse refers to false prophets who are filled with the spirit of antichrist. If we are genuine believers and followers of Jesus Christ, the Holy Spirit of God indwells us and is ready to release in us the power to live the Christian life, bear witness to Christ, and manifest the glory of God as never before. Jesus Himself promised:

> *You shall receive power when the Holy Spirit has come upon you; and you shall be witnesses to Me in Jerusalem, and in all Judea and Samaria, and to the end of the earth (Acts 1:8).*

Daniel 11:32 tells us that it is the people who truly know God who display strength and take action. Is it any wonder, then, that the devil takes his stand and fights against us so viciously? He knows who we are. Even more, he knows who we are becoming in Christ, and it terrifies him! Many of us don't realize that the devil is scared of us because we are children of God. He is, but that doesn't mean we should try to take him on one-on-one. In that kind of match-up, we will lose every time. Remember James's admonition: *"Therefore*

CHAPTER 8 – YOUR FAMILY'S DIVINE DESTINY

submit to God. Resist the devil and he will flee from you" (**James 4:7**). It is only as we submit ourselves to God in humble, childlike faith that He empowers us to resist the devil so successfully that he flees.

Let our quest be to so completely yield our minds to the illumination of the Holy Spirit that our whole way of looking at things is completely transformed. The Christian life is much more than doctrine and theology. Those things are important because we need to know what we believe and why, but apart from practical application, they are little more than intellectual knowledge. The Christian life is thoroughly practical. The Christian life is theology and doctrine in action. It is truth in action. It is love in action. The Christian life is the Word of God and the power of God together in action, in and through us on a daily basis, to bring in the Lord's harvest.

The key to all this is to have a spiritual mind that has been renewed in Christ. As we look to God to guide our way with His revelatory light, His Word will be a lamp to our feet and a light to our path (see **Ps. 119:105**). Why stumble around in the dark when we can walk in the light? Why muddle around in a mental fog when we can have the mind of Christ? Time is short. The harvest is plentiful, and everything is now ready. God is doing a new thing in the earth. We must stop listening to the lies of the devil and the life-limiting rhetoric of the world. We must not conform to this world, but be transformed by the renewing of our minds through the Holy Spirit. We must rid ourselves of any identity crisis and accept who we are—precious children of God! When we embrace who we are meant to be—anointed vessels of God, ordinary people through whom God wants to do extraordinary things—and grasp our divine destinies, we will began to realize that God's plans include our entire family line. Yes, we are destined to be super-overcomers and history makers. Arise shine be the beacon of hope to a hurting world, shine bright to your world.

Finally, brethren, whatever things are true, whatever things are noble, whatever things are just, whatever things are pure, whatever things are lovely, whatever things are of good report, if there is any virtue and if there is anything praiseworthy—meditate on these things
(Phil. 4:8).

CHAPTER 9

Building Identity Stability Will Instill Courage in Your Children

Overcome Your Identity Crisis

As I stated earlier, Heaven and hell are both posing the *same* question to every person in the Body of Christ. The Spirit of God and the devil are both asking us, *"Who do you think you are?"* It is an apt question, and the eternal destiny of millions rides on the answer. Saints of all ages struggle daily with their spiritual identity. Confused, they are tossed to and fro with no idea of who they are in Christ and little or no scriptural knowledge to give them a solid foundation. Such unawareness in a child of God is not only tragic, but also dangerous. As God said, *"My people are destroyed for lack of knowledge" (Hos. 4:6a).*

The apostle Peter likewise warned us to, *"Be sober, be vigilant; because your adversary the devil walks about like a roaring lion, seeking whom he may devour. Resist him, steadfast in the faith..." (1 Pet. 5:8-9a).*

Satan loves to pounce on immature believers who lack knowledge because, if he can keep them in the dark as to who they really are, he can prevent them from overcoming and walking in victory. In the battlefield of our minds, the devil seeks to sow evil seeds of doubt about God, His love, and His character. At the same time, he seeks to overwhelm our spirits with mind-gripping fear. The adversary of our souls is unrelenting in his attacks on God and His Word. He understands that, if he can sow the seeds of doubt within our hearts, soon unbelief will sprout.

Satan's very first words to humankind, as recorded in Genesis 3:1, were when he asked Eve, *"Has God indeed said, 'You shall not eat of every tree of the garden'?"* So very subtly, satan sowed a seed of doubt in Eve's mind that suggested that God was holding out on her and that God's plans and purposes for her were not best. The devil continues to use that same strategy today. He casts shadows of doubt in our minds regarding the certainty of the Word and the heart of God in an effort to make us think that God is not playing straight with us. But the goodness and integrity of God should never be in doubt: *"The Lord is good, a stronghold in the day of trouble; and He knows those who trust in Him"* **(Nah. 1:7)**; *"Oh, taste and see that the Lord is good; blessed is the man who trusts in Him" (Ps. 34:8).*

Our minds set the course and direction for our whole lives: *"For as he thinks in his heart, so is he"* **(Prov. 23:7a).** This being the case, it is vitally important that we fill our minds with the promises of God, such as **Micah 3:8:** *"But truly I am full of power by the Spirit of the Lord, and of justice and might..."* and **Second Timothy 1:7:** *"For God has not given us a spirit of fear, but of power and of love and of a sound mind."* The key to getting our heads on straight is filling our minds with the right kind of thoughts. Think about the right kind of things; as Paul says:

> *Finally, brethren, whatever things are true, whatever things are noble, whatever things are just, whatever things are pure, whatever things are lovely, whatever things are of good report, if there is any virtue and if there is anything praiseworthy—meditate on these things (Phil. 4:8).*

My high school football coach taught me a principle to aid me in bringing down the ball carrier: "The body will always follow the head." The same is true in our spiritual lives. If our minds are filled with wrong desires, we will waste our lives trying to satisfy them. On the other hand, if we set high and noble standards for our thoughts and lives, God will help us meet them because, ***"The steps of a good man are ordered by the Lord, and He delights in his way" (Ps. 37:23).***

We can achieve this upright life only by yielding control of our lives to the Holy Spirit. This requires that we die to self, self-will, and self-rule so that we can live to God, an act that Paul calls a "living sacrifice":

> ***I beseech you therefore, brethren, by the mercies of God, that you present your bodies a living sacrifice, holy, acceptable to God, which is your reasonable service (Rom. 12:1).***

Our hearts, minds, and spirits will never be free as long as we think and walk according to the flesh. We will realize our freedom in Christ only as we learn to walk by the Spirit of God. As Paul assures us:

> ***There is therefore now no condemnation to those who are in Christ Jesus, who do not walk according to the flesh, but***

according to the Spirit. For the law of the Spirit of life in Christ Jesus has made me free from the law of sin and death (Rom. 8:1-2).

And again Paul admonishes us:

I say then: Walk in the Spirit, and you shall not fulfill the lust of the flesh (Gal. 5:16).

If we allow the Holy Spirit to guide our thoughts and our steps, He will bring great grace to our lives. Only then will we be truly free to become all that God has purposed for us to be.

If we are going to change our lifestyles, we must first change our mindsets. We need a true "brain-washing" in order to rid ourselves of "stinking thinking." Our minds need to be thoroughly cleansed of the lies and filth of the world so that we can take up the mind of Christ, learning to think as He thinks and to see as He sees. A cleansed and renewed mind will completely change our perception of life and the world around us.

The Spirit of God is calling each of us to a higher standard, to *"walk worthy of the Lord, fully pleasing Him, being fruitful in every good work and increasing in the knowledge of God"* **(Col. 1:10).** This is not a season to be at ease and loose about our lifestyles. We must pursue peace and holiness, for without them we will not see the Lord (see **Hebrews 12:14**).

God calls all of His people to a life of purity, which is the path to holiness. Because He knows that sin in a person's life brings death and destruction pain and anguish.

As Paul wrote, *"Therefore, having these promises, beloved, let us cleanse ourselves from all filthiness of the flesh and spirit, perfecting holiness in the fear of God."*

2 Corinthians 7:1

This is a call to our complete consecration, in both body and spirit. In other words, we must figuratively lay down bodies and spirits as living sacrifices on the altar of God.

Leviticus 1:8 describes the process for consecrating a "voluntary offering" brought to the Lord by the people. The entire sacrificial animal— *"the parts, the head and the fat"*—was laid on the altar and burned completely. The fact that the animal's head was laid on the altar is significant for us because it reminds us that our minds must also be surrendered to the Lord for cleansing and consecrating, which is symbolized by the fire of the offering. It is with clean, consecrated minds that we enter into communion with the Lord.

A closer look at **Leviticus 1:8** reveals several prophetic insights: ***"Then the priests, Aaron's sons, shall lay the parts, the head, and the fat in order on the wood that is on the fire upon the altar."*** The name *Aaron* depicts "those who lift the light." Accordingly, we are called to be the light of the world, a city set upon a high hill that cannot be hidden (see **Matt. 5:14**).

The sacrificial animal was to be laid on the wood on the fire of the altar. It is only as the fire of God's Spirit falls upon us that we are truly empowered. In Acts chapter 2, the tongues of fire rested upon the heads of all in the upper room, and each one was filled with the Holy Spirit and with power.

There is an old gospel hymn, "Is Your All on the Altar," that says:

Is your all on the altar?

A sacrifice laid?

Your heart, does the Spirit control?

LINEAGE-LINE AND LEGACY

You can only be blessed

And have peace and sweet rest

As you yield Him your body and soul

It is time for us to lay our all on the altar and embrace the holy fire of God's presence! We must present minds that are clean and wholly consecrated to Him. Like David, our cry must be: *"Create in me a clean heart, O God, and renew a steadfast spirit within me"* **(Ps. 51:10).** When we do, we will discover that the Lord is transforming our worldly minds into spiritual minds—His mind.

Developing a Spiritual Mind

In the second chapter of his first letter to the Corinthians, the apostle Paul contrasted the natural mind and the spiritual mind. The natural mind, corrupted by sin, is dulled and darkened to spiritual things, however brilliant it may be in its own natural sphere. There are many intellectually brilliant people who haven't a clue regarding spiritual realities. They are *"always learning and never able to come to the knowledge of the truth"* **(2 Tim. 3:7).** Paul goes so far as to say that it is impossible for the natural mind to comprehend the things of the Spirit:

But the natural man does not receive the things of the Spirit of God, for they are foolishness to him; nor can he know them, because they are spiritually discerned.

1 Corinthians 2:14

It takes a spiritual mind to comprehend spiritual truth. As contradictory as it may seem, many true children of God are dominated still, for the most part, by the laws of their natural or carnal minds. One of the reasons the Church struggles so much today is because so many Christians still think like the world. And thoughts give birth to actions.

Some say, for example, "I won't believe it until I see it." This is the exact opposite of the spiritual mind. Jesus declared, in **John 11:40**, *"Did I not say to you that if you would believe you would see the glory of God?"* He spoke these words at the tomb of Lazarus in response to Martha's warning of the stench that would result if the tomb was opened as He had requested. Martha was looking and thinking from a carnal perspective. Jesus changed her viewpoint by raising her brother from the dead.

The natural mind says, "If I see, I will believe." The spiritual mind says, "If I believe, I will see."

Paul clearly recognized our desperate need for Spirit-enlightened minds, praying:

> *That the God of our Lord Jesus Christ, the Father of glory, may give to you the Spirit of wisdom and revelation in the knowledge of Him, the eyes of your understanding being enlightened; that you may know what is the hope of His calling, what are the riches of the glory of His inheritance in the saints.*
>
> *Ephesians 1:17-18*

Only in His light can we see light (see **Psalm 36:9**). We should cry out to God for spiritual eyes to see what we believe, even as we seek each day to walk in the light of His revealed Word. No matter how intellectually brilliant we may be, we cannot understand even the simplest concepts of God without the enlightenment of the Holy Spirit. The knowledge of spiritual things does not come by intellectual effort. Rather, it comes only by divine revelation. This is why, when Peter declared to Jesus, *"You are the Christ, the Son of the living God,"* Jesus said to him, *"Blessed are you, Simon Bar-Jonah, for flesh and blood has not revealed this to you, but My Father who is in Heaven"* (Matt. 16:16-17).

God's desire for all of His children is that they would possess and use a spiritual mind. That capacity already resides in each of us through the indwelling Holy Spirit. What Jesus said to His disciples applies also to us: ***"Blessed are your eyes for they see, and your ears for they hear"*** **(Matthew 13:16)**. Those who want to cultivate their spiritual minds must immerse themselves in the Word of God.

Hopefully you are one who longs to strengthen your spiritual mind. To do so, pray for revelation. Ask the Spirit of God to open your eyes to behold awesome things from God (see **James 1:5**). There is nothing wrong with intellectual knowledge and pursuit; God gave us our minds and expects us to use them. However, we should never depend upon our mere human intellectual wisdom to advance us in the realm of the Holy Spirit. Only upon the humble, spiritually-minded people of childlike faith does God impart great grace and release a powerful anointing.

Arise, shine; for your light has come! And the glory of the Lord is risen upon you. For behold, the darkness shall cover the earth, and deep darkness the people; but the Lord will arise over you, and His glory will be seen upon you. The Gentiles shall come to your light, and kings to the brightness of your rising. Lift up your eyes all around, and see: they all gather together, they come to you; your sons shall come from afar, and your daughters shall be nursed at your side. Then you shall see and become radiant, and your heart shall swell with joy; because the abundance of the sea shall be turned to you, the wealth of the Gentiles shall come to you.

(Isa. 60:1-5)

CHAPTER 10

Advance With Boldness Into Your Future

"No Hesitation"

Our first step toward victory is changing our attitudes and deciding to stop seeing ourselves as defenseless victims. Instead, we must see ourselves as victorious overcomers who are advancing with confidence and boldness (see **Romans 8:37**). The Spirit of God is encouraging each of us to change our attitude of defeat into an attitude of faith to advance. Like Joshua, we are commanded to be ***"strong and very courageous"* (Josh. 1:7)** as we move in power to take the Kingdom for the King! This is a season of no compromise for the Body of Christ! We are to walk with clean hands and pure hearts, drawing ever closer to our Lord.

The cry has gone forth: "No hesitation!" We must rise up, walking in dominion power and laying hold of the promises of God. This is not a time to be weak and waffling, but rather a time to be extremely bold and brave. No matter what the Lord has called us to do, He will not leave us alone to do it in our own strength. He will empower us and go before us, just as He went before the Israelites in a pillar of cloud by day and a pillar of fire by night (see **Exod. 13:21**).

We must listen with our whole hearts and take courage! God has promised victory, and He has called us to be the head and not the tail (see **Deut. 28:13**). We can be confident that victory is ours because His power is greater than the world's power: *"You are of God, little children, and have overcome them, because He who is in you is greater than he who is in the world"* **(1 John 4:4)**. We were created for victory; now is the time for us to shake ourselves and declare the proclamation found in **Micah 3:8a:** *"Truly I am full of power by the Spirit of the Lord!"*

We are in the harvest of the end of the ages— when both the seeds of good and evil are coming to full fruit. As Jesus said, the Kingdom of Heaven suffers violence, and the violent take it by force (see **Matt. 11:12**). Yet God is calling us to arise and take a strong stand against the works of darkness. We are to be bold, brave, and very courageous as we take the land for Jesus. This victory will be accomplished by individuals, as well as by the Church, the corporate Body of Christ, because the end-time Church will be a people of demonstrated power (see **1 Cor. 2:1-5**). It is time for the world to see a true demonstration of the power of God's Spirit. The cry has come up before the throne of God, *"Oh, that You would rend the heavens! That you would come down!"* (**Isa. 64:1a**).

Let us join with the plea of **Psalm 90:16-17:**

Let Your work appear to Your servants, and Your glory to their children. And let the beauty of the Lord our God be upon us, and establish the work of our hands for us; yes, establish the work of our hands.

The Church should be hungry and desperate to see the works of the Lord. We should long for Him to establish the works of our hands—His work in the world. I am weary of seeing the plans and purposes of people; I long to see the mighty acts of God! The Spirit of Truth is calling for us to come into the presence of the Lord. The way is clear, and any believer can advance higher. God has extended an open invitation for all who will to *"Come up here"* (**Rev. 4:1**), to enter the door that is standing open in Heaven so that we can see more clearly and hear more plainly. Doing so will equip us to advance ever deeper in the anointing, making the most of our divine call.

Paul instructed us to *"walk circumspectly, not as fools but as wise, redeeming the time, because the days are evil"* **(Eph. 5:15-16).** This means walking with the clear goal and aim of fulfilling God's divine purpose. This is not the time for us to wander around the mountain of defeat and unbelief. No! We are to lay hold of the promises of God, take Him at His Word, and stand firm in our faith.

One day God released to me this very encouraging statement: "This will be the season when My people begin to believe what they know. My word will move from the head to the heart to the hands." We will become doers of the Word, no longer content to simply be hearers. God has destined us to walk in victory, not defeat. We are called to be overcomers, not to be overcome. Remember, God has promised that no weapon formed against us can prosper (see **Isa. 54:17**).

Today the Body of Christ stands poised on the verge of the greatest move of God in the history of humankind. Accordingly, each of us should expect swift and radical change, swift and sure shifting. We do not have the time for another trip around the mountain; we must enter into the promises of God today.

No matter how confused and confounded we have been in the past, we now can personally begin to cease from our wilderness wanderings and begin to walk in our purpose of seeking first the Kingdom of God (see **Matt. 6:33**).

Paul prayed that we would *"walk worthy of the Lord, fully pleasing Him, being fruitful in every good work and increasing in the knowledge of God"* (**Col. 1:10**). Our highest goal must be to advance the King in His Kingdom. Our prayer each day must be, *"...Your will be done on earth as it is in Heaven"* (**Matt. 6:10**).

A swift synchronization of our walk to Heaven's will is needed. Just as Christ could say, **"I only do that which I see My Father doing"** (see **John 5:19),** we too must have clear focus. No higher commendation could be given than hearing our Father declare,

> *"Well done, good and faithful servant; you were faithful over a few things, I will make you ruler over many things. Enter into the joy of your Lord"* (**Matt. 25:21**).

For this reason, it is imperative that we maintain a deep walk in *the Word of God*. This will bring about the freedom that we need to draw near to the Lord. We must approach His hill with clean hands and a pure heart (see **Ps. 24:4-6**). Each day, we must seek to draw ever nearer to Christ, yielding our wills ever more to His will. As we truly behold Him with an unveiled face, we will be changed into His likeness (see **2 Cor. 3:18**).

The blood of Christ has power to set humankind free from all bondage. The choice is ours—whether or not we want to walk in freedom. In the days to come, we will see a radical return to the message of the redemptive blood of Christ, which is able to cleanse all sin. Christ is calling His Church today to advance on every front—to walk in the Word, in His anointing, and in His power to overthrow the gates of hell and set the captives free.

Obey the Lord

The second key principle to walking in victory is *walking in obedience*. **Obey the Lord.** It's that simple. Many ask the question, "Why do so many believers live in a state of bondage and defeat?" One of the main reasons is because so many of us have left our first love. When this is the case, our first prayer must be a prayer of confession and repentance. Then our second prayer must be, "Lord, restore my passion for You!" Christ has provided overwhelming victory for us through His blood. Therefore, there is no need—or excuse—for us to continue living in defeat.

Victory, however, will require our dedication to overcoming strongholds. If we will reaffirm our faith and rededicate ourselves to radical obedience, we can leave defeat in the dust and start walking in life-long victory. The words of that old gospel hymn say it so well:

Trust and obey,

For there's no other way

To be happy in Jesus,

But to trust and obey.

One of the most important aspects of the Christian walk is learning to obey quickly the voice of the Spirit of God. Just hearing the Word (voice) of the Lord is not enough; doing it is what matters. Obedience assures us victory in the long run, even if we experience setbacks and hardships at times. Victory will be ours because the Victorious One abides within us.

Lineage-Line and Legacy

The word *obey* is one of the strongest words in the human language to indicate hearing. Obeying the voice of Jesus is the only true evidence that we have heard Him. If we do not obey, we might as well be deaf; the result is the same. In fact, lack of obedience is evidence of lack of faith. James said that faith without works is dead (see **James 2:26**), and Jesus warned, ***"Not everyone who says to Me, 'Lord, Lord,' shall enter the kingdom of Heaven, but he who does the will of My Father in Heaven"*** (**Matt. 7:21**). True faith is always revealed in obedience, which is why the word in the New Testament that is usually translated "faith" also means "faithfulness." Our faithfulness is measured by the degree of our obedience to our "prime directive" from Christ: ***"But seek first the Kingdom of God and His righteousness; and all these things shall be added to you"*** (**Matt. 6:33**).

Sadly, many Christians have spent too much of their lives in disorientation and defeat because they simply have not obeyed the Word of God. Only as we seek first the Kingdom and righteousness of God—His priorities—will we receive clear guidance and revelation, not to mention provision for all the practical necessities of life that the rest of the world sweats and labors and worries over. One source of many believers' confusion is that they try to walk in the light of their own sparks rather than in the light of God's revealed Word. They make vital decisions based on their own desires and other earthly, temporary matters instead of seeking first the purposes of God's Kingdom.

If we would base all of our decisions on seeking the purposes of His Kingdom first, everything else would be added to us—without struggle or stress. That's the force of the Lord's promise in **Matthew 6:33.** We would have nothing to be anxious about, knowing who our Source and Protector is. Obedience is the key to everything, but we must obey the right things, the will and Word of God.

There is no greater freedom, no greater peace, than that which results from living our lives dedicated to the Lord in all things. No matter what our past has been like, we must let our past stay in the past. God created us to be the head and not the tail. His plan is for us to be above and not below. Now is the time to walk in freedom—which is found in obedience.

Sow Righteous Seed

Walking in victory also depends on us sowing righteous seed every day. In clear view from my back door in the beautiful Blue Ridge Mountains of North Carolina is a huge apple orchard covering several hundred acres. What a joy it is to watch the trees bloom in the spring and bear delicious fruit in the fall. All this is the result of one man with a big dream.

John Chapman, also known as Johnny Appleseed, came through our region in Moravian Falls, North Carolina, using the apple to preach the gospel. He used to say that you could count the seeds in an apple, but that you could not count the apples in a seed. This whole region of the state is now covered in apple trees that supposedly originated from this evangelist who preached here more than two hundred years ago. Like Johnny Appleseed, we too have precious seeds to sow— our special grace gifts from God.

What seed is the Lord leading you to sow that will provide a harvest? Do not miss your opportunity to sow, or you will miss your opportunity to celebrate at harvest time. Your joy in the Lord will be proportionate to your investment in the Lord. Sow little and you reap little; sow much and you reap abundantly.

This law of sowing and reaping includes, but is not limited to, our use of money. According to

Scripture, every Christian's life should have such an overflow so that we can be a channel of blessing to all who are in need.

This is what Paul had in mind when he wrote to the Corinthians:

But this I say: He who sows sparingly will also reap sparingly, and he who sows bountifully will also reap bountifully. So let each one give as he purposes in his heart, not grudgingly or of necessity; for God loves a cheerful giver.

And God is able to make all grace abound toward you, that you, always having all sufficiency in all things, may have an abundance for every good work. As it is written:

"He has dispersed abroad, He has given to the poor; His righteousness endures forever." Now may He who supplies seed to the sower, and bread for food, supply and multiply the seed you have sown and increase the fruits of your righteousness, while you are enriched in every- thing for all liberality, which causes thanksgiving through us to God (2 Cor. 9:6-11).

LINEAGE-LINE AND LEGACY

This is part of our "Promised Land"—having such an abundance, so much more than we ourselves need, that it blesses and touches everyone around us. I'm not just talking about money or material goods, but also about faith, hope, love, healing, and every other dimension of life. But it begins with material things because, as the Lord Jesus said, we cannot be trusted with the true riches of the Kingdom if we do not learn how to handle earthly riches (see **Luke 16:11**). Even so, Christ's Kingdom is not of this world and neither are the true blessings of the Promised Land that we are seeking. They are something that we are to walk in and demonstrate in this life, but they are not of this world.

Many are not able to hear such things, believing them to be "negative" prophecies, but they are biblical prophecies. Even the rough times that lie ahead will not be very difficult for those who have built their houses on the Rock by hearing and obeying the words of the Lord. On the other hand, difficult days lie ahead for those who do not abide in Christ. The fear barometer is going to rise a few more points because the earth is going to be groaning and travailing, and the lawless are going to become even more ruthless. People who have given themselves over to darkness will fall into even greater darkness. As the darkness grows, however, the light of the glory of the Lord, which is coming upon His people, will grow even brighter, eventually dispersing the darkness entirely, until the earth is *"filled with the knowledge of the glory of the Lord, as the waters cover the sea"* **(Hab. 2:14)**.

I believe that as we advance in the Spirit, in these days that lie ahead, we will move closer and closer to the time when the prophecy of Isaiah will be fulfilled in the Body of Christ, just as it was first fulfilled with the coming of Jesus Himself:

Arise, shine; for your light has come! And the glory of the Lord is risen upon you. For behold, the darkness shall cover the earth, and deep darkness the people; but the Lord will arise over you, and His glory will be seen upon you. The Gentiles shall come to your light, and kings to the brightness of your rising.

Lift up your eyes all around, and see: they all gather together, they come to you; your sons shall come from afar, and your daughters shall be nursed at your side. Then you shall see and become radiant, and your heart shall swell with joy; because the abundance of the sea shall be

turned to you, the wealth of the Gentiles
shall come to you (Isa. 60:1-5).

We see here that, at the very time when "deep darkness" is coming upon the people of the earth, the glory of the Lord is coming upon His people. If we are building our lives on the Kingdom of God, which cannot be shaken, we will have nothing to fear from the things that are now coming and are soon to come upon the world. Rather, it will be a time for great rejoicing when the glory of the Lord appears upon His people. The greatest treasure that we could ever possess is the one we already have—the Lord with us. Great days and unparalleled opportunities lie ahead, so we must plan ahead by taking advantage of every chance that we have to sow good seeds of righteousness now.

Teach Your Children to Respect Authority

One of the great duties parents can do for their children is instill in them respect for themselves as well as respect for authority. Any believer who desires to walk in the anointing and experience on-going victory in daily living must have a proper and biblical respect for authority. First, we acknowledge Christ as Lord—Master—and as Head of His Body, the Church. That means that He has authority over us and that we are responsible to obey Him. Respect for authority and obedience go hand-in-hand.

The Holy Spirit is always working to mold us and make us more like Jesus. He is preparing us to fulfill God's purpose, the establishment of His Kingdom. The more we learn about the King and His Kingdom, the more we will learn the importance of respecting authority. A Kingdom is the realm that is under the king's authority. To be entrusted with authority from the Lord requires that one first be under the authority of the Lord. We must also willingly submit to the authority of those spiritual leaders whom the Lord has placed over us. Unless we learn proper respect for authority, rules, and order in the Body of Christ, we will be a great danger to ourselves and others if we are given—or grab—more authority. This definitely flies in the face of the way the world operates, and as we move closer to the Day of the Lord, we can expect this contrast to increase.

Authority, discipline, and rules are not necessarily legalism, although in the wrong hands, they can cross that line. In all my years in ministry, I have never yet met one person who carries significant spiritual authority who was not at some time subjected either to an extreme form of legalism or to some other form of overly controlling authority. One of the great examples of this in Scripture is King David. King Saul was the tool that God used to fashion David into the great king that he would become. How did David react to the authority in his life that was so unjust and had even been demonized? David honored Saul to the end, refusing to lift his own hand against the king, even after Saul had tried to kill him many times (see **1 Sam. 24: 26**).

David even rewarded the men who recovered Saul's body and gave him a proper burial. He then went to the completely unprecedented extreme of honoring Saul's remaining family (see **2 Sam. 2:1-7; 9:1-13**). This was the exact opposite of the way of kings in those times, who quickly slew the children of any rivals. But David was of a different spirit. It was David's great respect for authority, those who were "anointed of the Lord," that enabled the Lord to entrust him with such remarkable authority that he was even used to establish the throne that the King of kings would sit upon. The Lord Jesus Himself would be affectionately called "the Son of David."

With David as our shining example of the way to respect authority, let us consider these exhortations from Scripture concerning authority:

Let every soul be subject to the governing authorities. For there is no authority except from God, and the authorities that exist are appointed by God. Therefore whoever resists the authority resists the ordinance of God, and those who resist will bring judgment on themselves. For rulers are not a terror to good works, but to evil. Do you want to be unafraid of the authority? Do what is good, and you will have praise from the same. For he is God's minister to you for good. But if you do evil, be afraid; for he does not bear the sword in vain; for he is God's minister, an avenger to execute wrath on him who practices evil. Therefore you must be subject, not only because of wrath but also for conscience' sake. For because of this you also pay taxes, for they are God's ministers attending continually to this very thing. Render therefore to all their due: taxes to whom taxes are due, customs to whom customs, fear to whom fear, honor to whom honor

(Rom. 13:1-7)

It is worth remembering that the highest authority in Paul's world, at the time that he wrote these words, was Nero, who was one of the most corrupt, evil, and demented of the Caesars and the one who eventually ordered Paul's execution. Nowhere does it say to be in subjection only to the most righteous and just authorities, but rather to all authorities.

Many Christians today disqualify themselves from receiving more authority from God because of the way they disrespect civil authority in its many and diverse manifestations. Remember, it was because of David's high calling that he was subjected to such a great test with a cruel, demented king like Saul.

If you want to walk in great authority, learn first to walk humbly, faithfully, and obediently under authority.

A Better Way

There is an erosion of respect for authority taking place in our times. It seems to be fast becoming a veritable meltdown. This will happen before the end of this age, and it will be the primary cause for **"the great time of trouble" or "the great tribulation"** (see **Matt. 24:21**). However, regardless of how outrageous governments or the authorities become, those who will be trusted with the authority of the coming

Kingdom must in every way treat them with dignity and respect. This is "the Saul test."

Do not speak evil of your leaders. Do not disrespect the police, mayors, governors, or any others in authority, and teach respect for them to your children, beginning with respect for their teachers, principals, and so forth.

This does not mean that we cannot disagree with their policies or actions, and in the cases of teachers, this might include some of their teachings, but we must do it in the most respectful way possible. In First Timothy, Paul gives us a more positive approach to authority:

> *First of all, then, I urge that entreaties and prayers, petitions and thanksgivings, be made on behalf of all men, for kings and all who are in authority, in order that we may lead a tranquil and quiet life in all godliness and dignity (1 Tim. 2:1-2 NASB).*

Here Paul exhorted us to pray first of all for those in authority. In other words, it should be our primary prayer activity.

In contrast to the growing lawlessness, there is an emerging generation of spiritual leaders who will come forth in the opposite spirit. These are the ones who will preach the gospel of the Kingdom with power because they will have been found trustworthy to handle spiritual authority. The Gentile centurion understood the nature of authority and how having authority happened by being under authority. The Lord commended him as having greater faith than anyone whom He had found in Israel (see **Matt. 8:5-10**). This is what we must understand if we are going to be trusted with the authority that the Lord will give only to the trustworthy.

Before we consider a few simple things that we can do to combat this growing lawlessness, let us take time to think about what the Lord said about it in the following Scriptures:

> *Many will say to Me on that day, "Lord, Lord, did we not prophesy in Your name, and in Your name cast out demons, and in Your name perform many miracles?" And then I will declare to them, "I never knew you; depart from Me, you who practice lawlessness" (Matt. 7:22-23 NASB)*

No matter what type of gift we manifest or how spiritual and righteous we sound, if we do not truly know and follow the Lord, we will be rejected. In another place, Jesus gave another stern warning that is extremely clear:

> *The Son of Man will send forth His angels, and they will gather out of His kingdom all stumbling blocks, and those who commit lawlessness, and will cast them into the furnace of fire; in that place there shall be weeping and gnashing of teeth (Matt. 13:41-42 NASB).*

Harsh judgment will be rendered upon those who commit lawlessness and those who place stumbling blocks in the path of other followers or in the path of those who wish to follow. Particularly distasteful to the Lord are those who cloak their lawlessness in religious garb:

> *Woe to you, scribes and Pharisees, hypocrites! For you are like whitewashed tombs which on the out- side appear beautiful, but inside they are full of dead men's bones and all uncleanness. So you too outwardly appear righteous to men, but inwardly you are full of hypocrisy and lawlessness (Matt. 23:27-28 NASB).*

Even in the midst of rampant lawlessness, however, there is hope for the faithful: ***"Because*** *lawlessness is increased, most people's love will grow cold. But the one who endures to the end, he will be saved" (Matt. 24:12-13).*

Overcoming Lawlessness

Freedom does not mean that we are to live loosely. Rather, we must understand that, although we are not under the law, neither are we above it. We must submit ourselves to the Lord and respect His authority. As leaders, we must teach our children to do the same. If we do not teach our children to respect authority, we are not equipping them for what will, in all probability, be the major battle they will have to face in these times.

Remember why Abraham, the "father of faith," was chosen by God, as Genesis 18:19 tells us:

> *For I have chosen him, so that he may command his children and his household after him to keep the way of the Lord by doing righteousness and justice, so that the Lord may bring upon Abraham what He has spoken about him (Gen. 18:19 NASB).*

God said that He had chosen Abraham so that he would *"command his children...after him to keep the way of the Lord."* The very right of parents to exercise authority over their children is under increasing attack in these times. But we must prevail in this fight for the sake of our children. It is essential, however, that we do this in love rather than frustration, anger, or impatience.

We must also understand that sin is lawlessness, and impurity leads to lawlessness, as Paul tells us in Romans:

> ***I am speaking in human terms because of the weakness of your flesh. For just as you presented your members as slaves to impurity and to lawlessness, resulting in further lawlessness, so now present your members as slaves to righteousness, resulting in sanctification. For when you were slaves of sin, you were free in regard to righteousness. Therefore what benefit were you then deriving from the things of which you are now ashamed? For the outcome of those things is death. But now having been freed from sin and enslaved to God, you derive your benefit, resulting in sanctification, and the outcome, eternal life. For the wages of sin is death, but the free gift of God is eternal life in Christ Jesus our Lord (Rom. 6:19-23 NASB).***

Lawlessness, like faith, usually begins with a seed, which is then watered and cultivated, bringing forth sin, as described above. It often begins with impurity, which will always lead to lawlessness. Impurity and lawlessness are bound together, as John describes: *"And everyone who has this hope fixed on Him purifies himself, just as He is pure. Everyone who practices sin also practices lawlessness; and sin is lawlessness"* **(1 John 3:3-4 NASB).**

Finally, let us consider how we can comply with the exhortation of **Romans 13:8-14**, which follows Paul's exhortation to honor those who are in positions of authority:

Owe nothing to anyone except to love one another; for he who loves his neighbor has fulfilled the law. For this, "You shall not commit adultery, you shall not murder, you shall not steal, you shall not covet," and if there is any other commandment, it is summed up in this saying, "you shall love your neighbor as yourself." Love does no wrong to a neighbor; love therefore is the fulfillment of the law. Do this, knowing the time, that it is already the hour for you to awaken from sleep; for now salvation is nearer to us than when we believed. The night is almost gone, and the day is near. Therefore let us lay aside the deeds of darkness and put on the armor of light. Let us behave properly as in the day, not in carousing and drunkenness, not in sexual promiscuity and sensuality, not in strife and jealousy. But put on the Lord Jesus Christ, and make no provision for the flesh in regard to its lusts (Rom. 13:8-14 NASB).

Love, Not Legalism

God's response to lawlessness and rebellion is not legalism, but love. If we are growing in our love for God and for others, it will be the desire of our hearts to keep our hearts pure for them. Love is the fulfillment of the law, and love should be our motivation for teaching our children to love God and to respect authority. This is such a crucial issue in our times. The Church is in desperate need of true shepherds who have the Father's heart for His people, but few have been willing to submit to the process required to conform their hearts to His.

Do not waste the trials that come to you in whatever form—in the Church or in non-Church relationships with people at your job, in your family, within the civil government, and so forth. Like David, resolve to honor all who are in authority, and do not let bitterness or rejection find a place in your heart. **Ephesians 4:32** says, *"Be kind to one another, tenderhearted, forgiving one another, even as God in Christ forgave you."*

Don't worry that you're not a Christian "superstar." There's no such thing anyway. Those who walk in a powerful anointing are ordinary folk like you and me who got hungry and desperate for a fresh touch from the Lord and humbly submitted themselves to Him. Consequently, God has taken them in their ordinariness and humility and weakness, and He does extraordinary things through them. The truth is He wants to do the same with you. Submit yourself humbly to God. Advance boldly. Obey the Lord. Sow righteous seeds. Respect authority. Live righteously. Walk in these things, and not only will you walk in a powerful anointing, but you also will walk in victory all of the days of your life!

"Be kind to one another, tenderhearted, forgiving one another, even as God in Christ forgave you."
                                    Ephesians 4:32

CONCLUSION

Many years ago one of my schoolteachers would say to me this little motto that through the years has been a great motivating force for me. He said *"Bobby, always remember "Good!" – "Better!" – "Best!" never let it rest until your good is better and your better is best!"* Each of us must realize that in every area of our life there is always room for improvement.

I have a little plaque, which states: **"YES YOU CAN!"** This is sound, good advice for all of us. You and your family lines are important to the plans and purposes of God. The devil understands this, so he is busy attempting to devastate and destroy as many families and family lines as possible. Yet God has made the declaration, "I will restore, all that has been taken" (see **Joel 2:25**).

Bring your life back to Christ Jesus with a heart filled with repentance and ask for a fresh start, God will restore and refresh you (see **Isa. 1:18**). It is never too late for a complete turnaround. Let this be a time of great redemption and restoration for you and your family.

LINEAGE-LINE AND LEGACY

Starting this very day, make up your mind and make this life-changing declaration with **Joshua 24:15,** *"As for me and my house we will serve the Lord!"* It is at this point that everything changes for the good, for you as well as your lineage-line. This is why you must fight the good fight of faith for your family. *"Fight the good fight of faith, lay hold of eternal life, whereunto you are also called, and have professed a good profession before many witnesses"* **(1 Tim. 6:12 KJV).**

Live in such a manner that, in years to come, when your name is spoken, your lineage-line will beam with respect and hearts overflowing for the good, godly foundations set for them by your godly lifestyle.

Make it a personal goal to so conduct your life that you will hear your Heavenly Father say, "This is My beloved child, in whom I am well pleased!" Live in such an upright manner that the preacher will be able to tell the truth about you at your funeral.

I bless you on your quest to please the Father in all you say and do as you advance the King in His Kingdom. Here is my prayer for you and your entire family:

May the Lord give you increase more and more, You and your children. May you be blessed by the Lord, Who made heaven and earth.
Psalms 115:14-15

Blessings!

Bobby Conner

Eagles View Ministries

RESOURCES

BOBBY CONNER
EaglesViewMinistries

LIVING IN GOD'S LIGHT

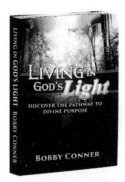

Within these pages you will discover inspirational insights; these truths have the potential to radically transform your life.

These life lessons will release hope and impart courage and confidence giving you guidelines revealing how to best position yourselves to obtain God's perfect plans and purposes for your life .

This book will aid you as a seeker of Divine Truth to dig ever deeper into the treasures of God's Word, thus obtaining the wonderful promises that will release to you steadfastness and confidence to face uncertain times .

RESOURCES

BOBBY CONNER
EaglesViewMinistries

EMPOWERED BY GOD

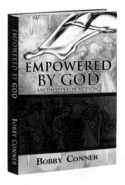

You are called and commissioned to walk in Kingdom authority and power! As a follower of Christ Jesus you are expected to accomplish the same supernatural works He did even greater.

This book will aid you in realizing how to embrace the process and purpose of spiritual character and maturity, the importance of investing your life into the kingdom.

It is time to exit the pathway of apathy and advance in the journey to divine empowerment becoming a spiritual revolutionary ready to shape the future!

BOBBY CONNER
EaglesViewMinistries
www.BobbyConner.org
PO BOX 933, BULLARD, TEXAS 75757